STEVE AND MEGUMI BIDDLE'S

STEP-BY-STEP

ORIGAMI

STEVE AND MEGUMI BIDDLE'S

STEP-BY-STEP
ORIGAMI

EBURY PRESS
London

First published by Ebury Press
an imprint of The Random Century Group
Random Century House
20 Vauxhall Bridge Road
London SW1V 2SA

British Library Cataloguing in Publication Data
Biddle, Steve
    Step-by-step origami: an easy-to-follow guide with over 1500 illustrations.
    1. Origami. Techniques
    I. Title   II. Biddle, Megumi
    736.982
    ISBN 0-85223-813-4 (paperback)
    ISBN 0-09-175060-1 (hardback)

Edited by Helen Southall and Jane Struthers
Designed by Bridgewater Design Limited

Typeset in Frutiger by Textype Typesetters, Cambridge
Printed in Hong Kong by L. Rex Offset Printing Co. Ltd

CONTENTS

INTRODUCTION

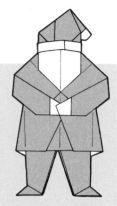

Welcome to the fabulous world of origami — the art of paper folding. Origami can be enjoyed by everybody, regardless of age, nationality and language. Nowadays in many parts of the world, people of all ages and from all sorts of backgrounds are folding paper for pleasure.

Step-by-Step Origami will introduce you to some of the traditional origami folds as well as many new ones. If you have never tried origami before, then this book is a good one to begin with. But if you are already accomplished at origami, we hope that you will be excited by the new folds in this book (many of which are featured for the first time).

To enjoy *Step-by-Step Origami*, you will find it easiest to work your way through from beginning to end, as many of the folds and folding procedures are based partially on previous ones. Therefore we suggest that you start at the beginning and don't jump backwards and forwards unless, of course, you can follow origami instructions without too much help.

This book has been designed to take you, the folder, from the very first, easy steps, to the much more intricate methods used to produce many original types of origami. In this way you will discover the greater pleasure of creating more complex folds of your own by using the techniques you have already learned.

You may be wondering what sort of paper to use. Most of the models in this book are folded from a square of paper, although in a few cases you will need more than just one. All kinds of paper can be folded into origami, but do try to find a paper that suits you best. Packets of origami paper, coloured on one side and white on

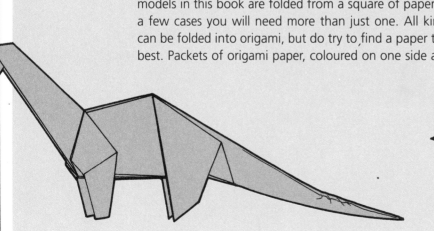

the other, can be obtained from department stores, toy shops, stationery shops and oriental gift shops. Other papers suitable for origami can be found in art and craft shops. Why not try using the fancy gift wrapping papers that are now widely available? You could even cut out a few pages from a colour magazine! Your paper does not have to be coloured on one side, but it can help to make the finished origami look very attractive.

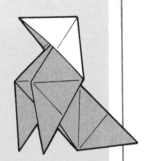

We would like to thank the members of the Nippon Origami Association (NOA) for sharing their ideas with us. NOA was founded in 1973 to bring together scholars, teachers, representatives and top artists of the origami world with the following objectives:

- To spread peace and friendship through origami and to make origami a symbol of peace.
- To spread the enjoyment of working with origami, which stimulates creativity and the pleasure of making things.
- To preserve origami throughout the world.

We would very much like to hear from you about your interest in origami, or if you have any problems in obtaining origami materials. So please write to us, care of our publishers (the address is on page 4 of this book), enclosing a stamped addressed envelope.

Finally, we would like to echo the words of our very good origami friends, Lillian Oppenheimer of New York City and Toshie Takahama of Tokyo, Japan: always remember that the real secret of origami lies in the giving and sharing with others. We do hope you have a lot of fun in discovering the limitless possibilities of origami.

STEVE AND MEGUMI BIDDLE

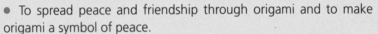

HELPFUL TIPS

Before you try any of the procedures or projects in this book, here are some very helpful tips that will make origami easier:

● Fold on a smooth flat surface, such as a table or a book.
● Make your folds neat and accurate.
● Press your folds into place by running your thumb nail along them.
● In the diagrams, the shading represents the coloured side of the paper.
● Try to take great care in obtaining the right kind of paper to match the origami that you plan to fold. This will help to enhance the finished product.
● Before you start, make sure your paper is square.

● Do not panic if your first few attempts at folding are not very successful. With practice you will come to understand the many ways in which a piece of paper behaves when it is folded.
● Look at each diagram carefully, read the instructions and look ahead at the same time to the next diagram to see what shape will be created as the result of the step you are working on.
● Above all, if a fold or a whole model does not work out, do not give up hope. Go through all the diagrams one by one, checking that you have read the instructions correctly and have not missed an important word or overlooked a symbol. If that does not work, put the fold to one side and come back to it another day with a fresh mind.

SYMBOLS AND FOLDING PROCEDURES

The symbols used in this book have been developed by the Nippon Origami Association, and it is important that you understand them as they show you the direction in which the paper has to be folded. So, look very carefully at the diagrams to see which way the dashes, dots and arrows go over, through, and under, and fold your paper accordingly.

If you are new to origami and are folding for the first time, you may be worried about mastering all the paperfolding jargon. We therefore suggest that, before trying the many origami projects, you take a few squares of paper and study the following symbols and procedures. In this way you will get to know the most basic points about origami and, after spending a few minutes learning them, you will be able to fold from almost any book on origami, even if you cannot understand the language in which it is written.

VALLEY FOLD

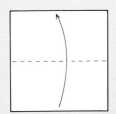

1 This is the simplest and most common technique to be found in origami. A valley fold (fold forwards or in front) is shown by a line of dashes and a solid arrow showing the direction in which the paper has to be folded.

2 Hold down the top edge of a square of paper. Lift the bottom edge up . . .

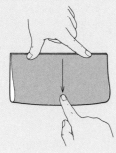

3 and bring it up to meet the top edge. Keeping the edges together, run your forefinger down the middle of the paper to the bottom edge.

4 Run your forefinger along the bottom edge to both sides, thereby completing the fold. If you turn the paper sideways on and unfold it a little, you can see the shape resembles a valley, hence the name of this fold.

MOUNTAIN FOLD

1 A mountain fold (fold backwards or behind) is shown by a line of dots and dashes (usually a long dash followed by two dots) and a hollow-headed arrow. As in the valley fold, the arrow always shows the direction in which the paper has to be folded.

2 Hold the bottom of a square of paper. Bend the top edge backwards . . .

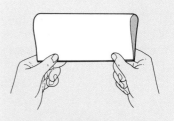

3 and take it down to meet the bottom edge.

4 Keeping the edges together, run your thumb up the middle of the paper to the top edge. Run your thumb and fingers along the top edge, thereby completing the fold. If you turn the paper sideways on and unfold it a little, you can see the shape resembles a mountain.

FOLD AND UNFOLD

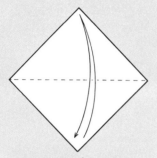

1 An arrow which comes back on itself means 'Fold, press flat and unfold the paper back to its previous position'.

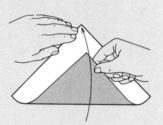

2 Turn a square of paper around to look like a diamond. Valley fold it in half from bottom to top, thereby making a triangle. Press it flat.

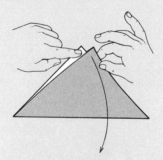

3 Unfold the triangle completely.

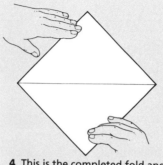

4 This is the completed fold and unfold. A faint, solid line represents an existing fold-line, i.e. one that is the result of a previous step.

FOLD OVER AND OVER

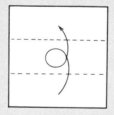

1 A looped arrow drawn on top of the diagram means 'Fold the paper over and over again in the direction shown by the arrow'. Each fold-line represents one fold-over move.

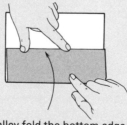

2 Valley fold the bottom edge of a square of paper up to a point that is about one-third of the distance to the top edge.

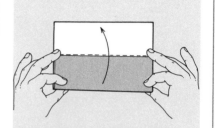

3 Valley fold the bottom 'folded' edge up to meet the top edge.

4 Press the paper flat, thereby completing the fold over and over technique.

STEP FOLD

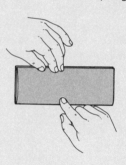

1 A zigzagged arrow drawn on top of the diagram means 'Fold the paper in the direction shown by the arrow'. A step fold is made by pleating the paper in a valley and mountain fold, so it becomes like a step.

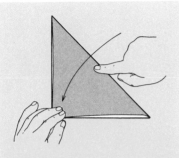

2 Valley fold a square of paper in half from top right to bottom left, thereby making a triangle.

3 From the bottom left-hand corner, valley fold the top layer of paper up, so . . .

4 it lies over the triangle's longest side. Press it flat, thereby completing the step fold.

INSIDE REVERSE FOLD

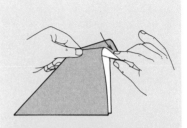

1 Inside reverse folds are very easy to do and, after valley and mountain folds, they are the most commonly used technique in origami. An inside reverse fold is shown by a wavy-headed arrow and a mountain fold-line.

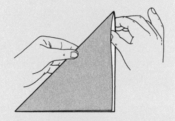

2 Valley fold a square of paper in half from top left to bottom right, to make a triangle. Insert your thumb between the right-hand layers of paper and at the same time place your forefinger on the triangle's ridge as shown.

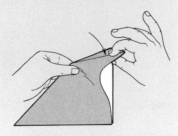

3 Draw back your forefinger and at the same time push down on the ridge, . . .

4 thereby changing it into a valley fold.

5 Press the paper flat, thereby completing the inside reverse fold. This technique is so named because the paper being folded moves inside and a ridge is reversed from a mountain to a valley fold. You can prepare for an inside reverse fold by valley folding the paper at the required angle, pressing it flat and returning it to its original position. Using the fold-lines you have just made, it is now easy to make an inside reverse fold.

OUTSIDE REVERSE FOLD

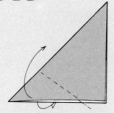

1 An outside reverse fold is also very easy, but it does require a little preparation beforehand. An outside reverse fold is shown by solid and hollow-headed arrows and valley and mountain fold-lines.

2 Valley fold a square of paper in half from top left to bottom right, to make a triangle. Valley fold its bottom left-hand point over at the required angle.

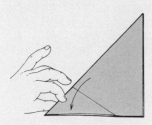

3 Press the point flat, then unfold it.

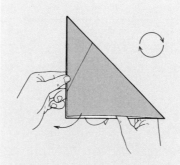

4 Turn the paper around. The new symbol of two circling arrows means 'Turn the paper around into the position as shown in the diagram'. Separate the layers of paper, . . .

5 taking one to the front and one to the back.

6 Press down on the fold-lines made in step 3, to convert them into valley folds, at the same time . . .

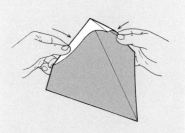

7 bringing the top point forwards.

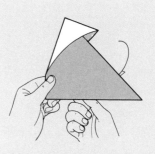

8 Mountain fold the paper in half along the middle.

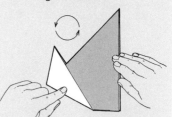

9 Turn the paper around and press it flat, thereby completing the outside reverse fold. This technique is so named because the paper being folded moves outside the rest of the paper and the fold-lines are reversed into valley folds.

CUT

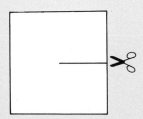

1 A pair of scissors and a solid line means 'Cut the paper'.

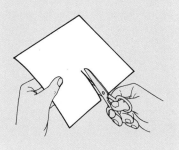

2 The solid line shows the position of the cut.

TURN OVER

1 A looped arrow means . . .

2 'Turn the paper . . .

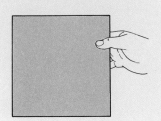

3 over in the direction shown'.

ENLARGE

A swollen arrow with a pointed tail shows that the following diagram is drawn to a larger scale.

INSERT

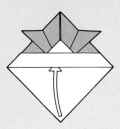

A hollow arrow with a long tail means 'Insert'. This symbol is used when a flap or point has to be inserted, either into a pocket or underneath a layer of paper.

OPEN AND SQUASH

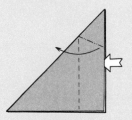

1 The open and squash technique is not at all tricky to do. As open and squash folds can come in many shapes and disguises, it is important to learn this technique carefully. An open and squash is shown by a hollow arrow with a short, indented tail.

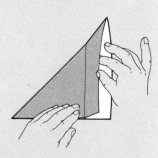

2 Valley fold a square of paper in half from top left to bottom right, to make a triangle. Valley fold its right-hand side over towards the left (its exact position is not important). Press the side flat and lift it up along the fold-line that has just been made. Insert your fingers between the layers of paper.

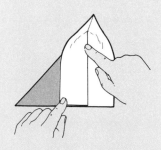

3 Start to open out the layers and, with your other hand, . . .

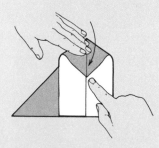

4 squash them down neatly into this shape. Press the paper flat, thereby completing the open and squash technique. This technique is so named because layers of paper or a pocket have been opened out and squashed down.

PULL OUT

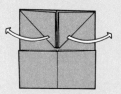

Two hollow arrows, both with long tails, mean 'Pull out'. These symbols are used when layers of paper or points have to be pulled out in a certain direction.

BLOW UP

A hollow arrow with a balloon-like tail means 'Blow up'. This symbol is used when a particular fold has to be inflated. The arrow's head will show the place into which you must blow.

SIMPLE ORIGAMI FOLDS

In origami, a few folded shapes are used. Each shape is called a fold, and more often than not its name is descriptive. As origami is all about folding paper, let us start with the simplest of folds, the book fold. This fold is also the foundation of the cupboard fold. These basic folds can be used to make a number of simple origami models.

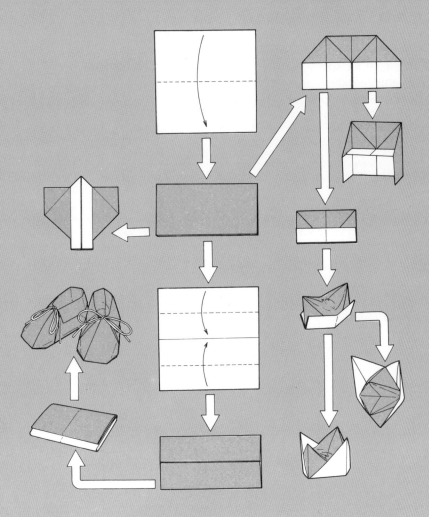

BOOK FOLD *(Traditional)*

The book fold is so named because, once the paper is folded in half, it resembles a book.

Use a square of paper, white side up.

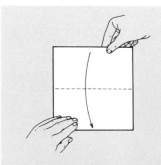

1 Valley fold the square in half from top to bottom.

2 Press the paper flat, thereby completing the book fold. A book fold can also be made by valley folding a square in half from side to side.

CUPBOARD FOLD *(Traditional)*

By using the book fold as our foundation we are able to develop another fold from it called the cupboard fold. It is so named because once the paper is folded it resembles a cupboard with two doors that can be opened and closed.

Use a square of paper, white side up.

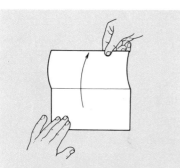

1 Begin with a book fold. Unfold it completely.

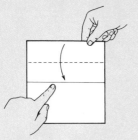

2 Valley fold the top edge down to meet the middle fold-line.

3 Press the paper flat.

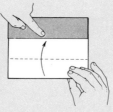

4 Valley fold the bottom edge up to meet the middle fold-line.

5 Press the paper flat, thereby completing the cupboard fold.

FAMILY FOLDS *(Traditional)*

This series of folds is an ideal example of how one can build up a whole range of models, each one leading into the other, by making just a few slight changes in the folding steps. These models are also perfect examples of what can be made by combining two folds, in this example the book and cupboard folds.

For each model use a square of paper, white side up.

HOUSE

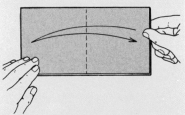

1 Begin with a book fold (see opposite). Valley fold it in half from side to side. Press it flat and unfold it.

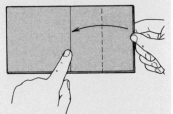

2 Valley fold the right-hand side over to meet the middle fold line.

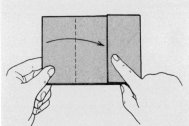

3 Repeat step 2 with the left-hand side.

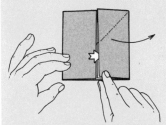

4 Lift the right-hand side up.

5 Insert your fingers between the layers of paper. Open them out and, . . .

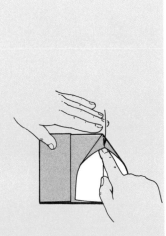

6 with your free hand, squash down the top into the shape of a triangular roof. Press the paper flat.

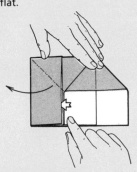

7 Repeat steps 4 to 6 with the left-hand side, thereby completing . . .

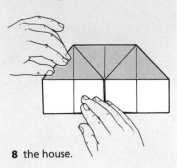

8 the house.

ORGAN

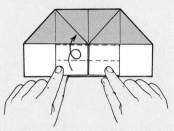

9 Begin with a completed step 8, the house. Fold over and over the bottom edge of the centre panel.

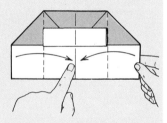

10 Valley fold the sides over to meet the middle fold-line.

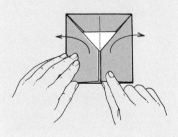

11 Unfold the sides so they stand upright.

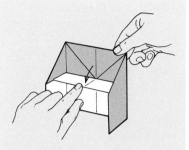

12 Pull down the centre panel, thereby completing the organ.

PAPER HAT

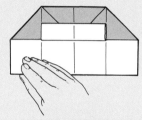

13 Begin with a completed step 9, the organ.

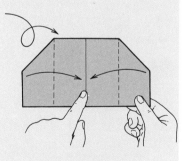

14 Turn the paper over. Valley fold the sides over to meet the middle fold-line.

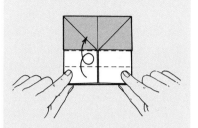

15 Fold over and over the bottom edge.

16 Open the paper out along the bottom edge. The new symbol of a solid arrow with a very short tail means 'Apply pressure to this folded edge'.

17 Insert your fingers inside the paper. As you do so, push the top in a little, thereby completing the paper hat. To make an origami hat that you can wear, use a square of paper that is the same size as one made from a broadsheet (large-sized) newspaper.

FOX PUPPET

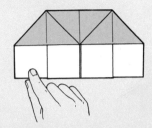

18 Begin with a completed step 8, the house.

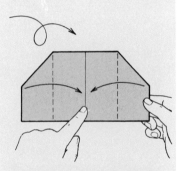

19 Turn the paper over. Valley fold the sides over to meet the middle fold-line.

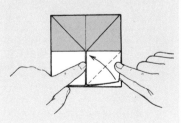

20 Valley fold the bottom right-hand corner into the middle.

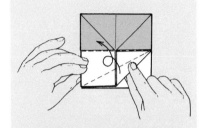

21 Valley fold the top layer of paper up on a line between the bottom left-hand corner and the middle of the right-hand side. Now valley fold the . . .

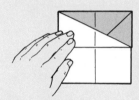

22 left-hand corner of the same layer up to meet the top edge. Press the paper flat.

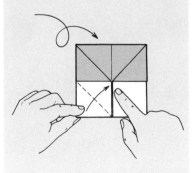

23 Turn the paper over. Valley fold the bottom left-hand corner into the middle.

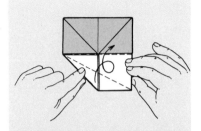

24 Repeat step 21, valley folding on a line between the bottom right-hand corner and the middle of the left-hand side. Finally, valley fold the right-hand corner up to meet the top edge. Press the paper flat.

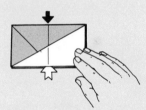

25 Open the paper out along the bottom edge.

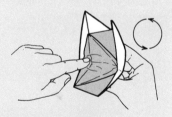

26 To complete the fox, turn the paper around, insert your thumb and forefinger inside, and as you do so push the top in a little, so that on the inside you make a diagonal centre division. To make the fox 'talk', rest him on the back of your free hand and move the forefinger that is inside him up and down.

CROWN

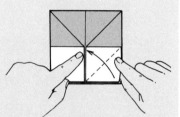

27 Begin with a completed step 19. Valley fold the bottom right-hand corner into the middle.

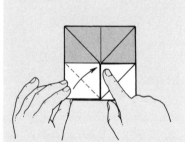

28 Valley fold the bottom left-hand corner into the middle.

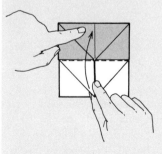

29 Valley fold the middle point up to meet the top edge.

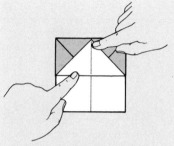

30 This should be the result. Press the paper flat.

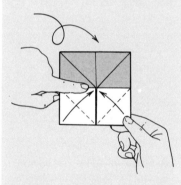

31 Turn the paper over. Valley fold the two bottom corners into the middle.

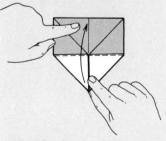

32 Valley fold the bottom point up to meet the top edge. Press the paper flat.

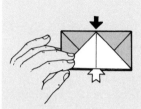

33 Open the paper out along the bottom edge. As you do so, push the top in . . .

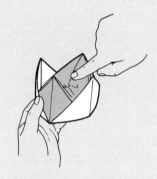

34 and shape it into place, thereby completing the crown.

HAPPI COAT *(Traditional)*

Watch out for the open and squash move that appears towards the end. By varying the position of the valley fold in step 2 you can make the happi coat larger or smaller.

Use a square of paper, white side up.

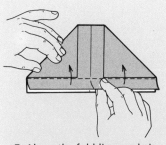

5 Along the fold-line made in step 2, valley fold a single layer of paper up from the bottom.

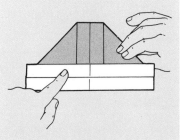

6 Press the paper flat.

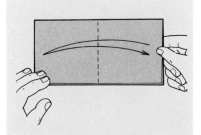

1 Begin with a book fold (see page 16). Valley fold it in half from side to side. Press it flat and unfold it.

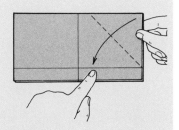

3 Valley fold the top right-hand corner down as shown, so it meets the fold-line already made in step 2.

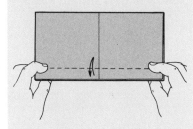

2 Treating them as if they were one, valley fold a little of the two bottom edges up. (The exact position of this fold is not important.) Press them flat and unfold them.

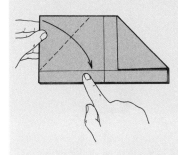

4 Repeat step 3 with the top left-hand corner.

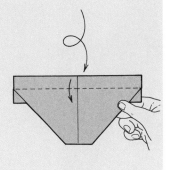

7 Turn the paper over. Along the fold-line made in step 2, valley fold the remaining layer of paper down from the top.

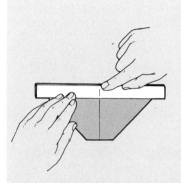

8 Press the paper flat.

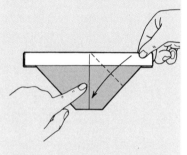

9 Valley fold the right-hand half of the top edge down to meet the middle fold-line.

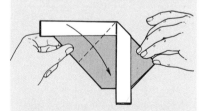

10 Repeat step 9 with the left-hand half of the top edge.

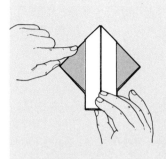

11 Press the paper flat.

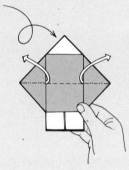

12 Turn the paper over. Here comes the open and squash move. This is what you do. . . .

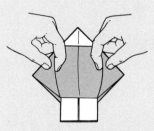

13 Insert your fingers into the right- and left-hand triangular pockets of paper.

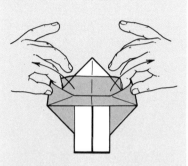

14 Carefully pull the pockets out to either side, at the same time . . .

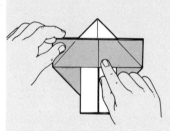

15 squashing and pressing them down neatly into this position.

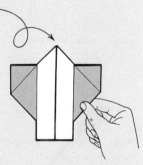

16 Turn the paper over, thereby completing the happi coat.

PURSE *(Traditional)*

This delightful piece of origami is made by folding three simple units which are then fitted together. Use three squares of paper, identical in size.

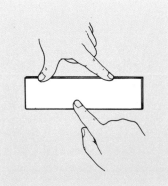

5 Press the paper flat.

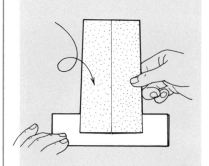

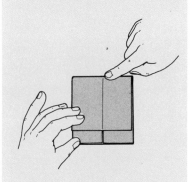

3 that is slightly short of the bottom edge. It is important to leave a short space at the bottom, otherwise in step 11 you will not be able to lock the units together.

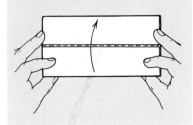

4 Unit B: turn another cupboard fold around, so it is sideways on. Valley fold it in half from bottom to top.

6 Unit C: turn the remaining cupboard fold over, so its 'doors' are face down. Place it centrally on to the top of unit B.

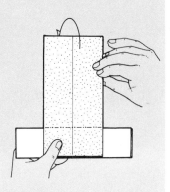

7 Mountain fold unit C down and along the top edge of unit B.

1 Begin by folding each of the squares into a cupboard fold (see page 16).

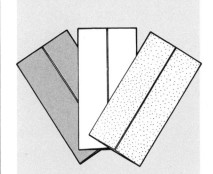

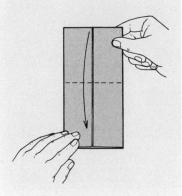

2 Unit A: turn one cupboard fold around, so it is lengthways on. Valley fold the top edge down to a point . . .

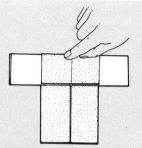

8 This should be the result.

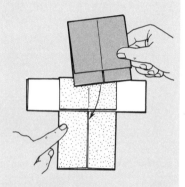

9 Place unit A on top of units B and C as shown.

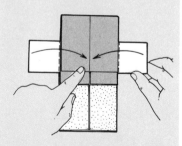

10 Carefully note the position of unit A's short space. Valley fold the sides of unit B over unit A.

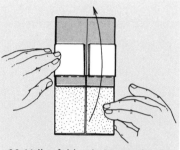

11 Valley fold unit C up and over units A and B as shown, thereby locking them all together.

12 Tuck what is left of unit C . . .

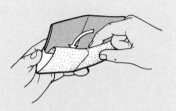

13 down inside the model, by going between the front and back layers of paper.

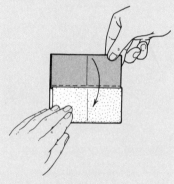

14 Valley fold what is left of unit A down and over the top of the model.

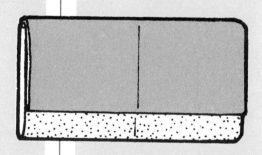

15 Here is the completed purse.

BABY'S SHOES *(Katsushi Nosho)*

With this piece of origami try to make your folds as neat and accurate as possible. The novel twist to this model is that it is held together with a bow, just like a real shoe.

Use a 15 cm (6 in) square of paper, white side up. You will also need a 25 cm (10 in) length of string.

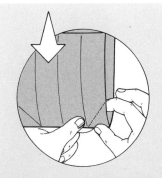

5 Holding the paper with your left hand, insert your right forefinger between the layers as shown. With your right thumb . . .

1 Begin with a cupboard fold (see page 16). Turn it around so it is lengthways on. Valley fold the sides over to meet the vertical middle line. Press them flat and unfold them.

3 Valley fold the bottom right-hand corner up to meet the adjacent fold-line. Press it flat and unfold it. Repeat this step with the bottom left-hand corner.

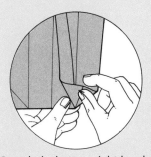

6 push the bottom right-hand corner up and . . .

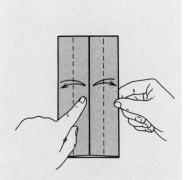

2 Valley fold the paper in half from bottom to top.

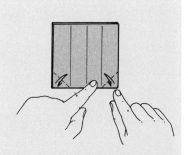

4 Inside reverse fold the bottom corners. This is what you do. . . .

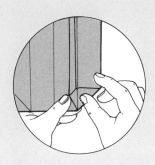

7 inside the model along the fold-lines made in step 3.

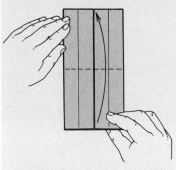

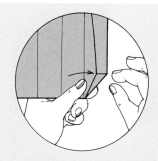

8 To complete, press the paper flat.

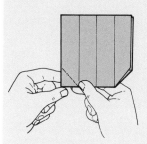

9 Now inside reverse fold the bottom left-hand corner.

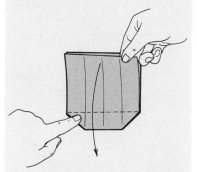

10 Valley fold the topmost layer of paper down on the horizontal line that runs along the top edge of the reversed corners.

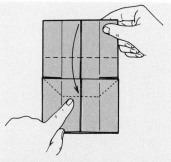

11 Valley fold the top layer of paper down as far as shown. The new symbol of a series of dotted lines shows what the paper is like underneath. This symbol means 'X-ray view'.

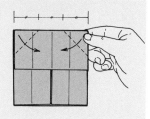

12 Valley fold the top right-hand corner down to a point one-third of the distance to the opposite side. Repeat this step with the top left-hand corner. The new symbol above this step means 'These distances are equal'.

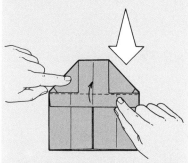

13 Valley fold the middle flap of paper up and over the triangles.

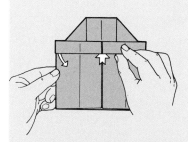

14 Slightly lift the top layer of paper up and release the left-hand side from the point where it is 'caught'.

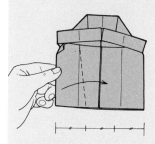

15 On a slant, valley fold the left-hand side over to a point one-third of the distance to the opposite side.

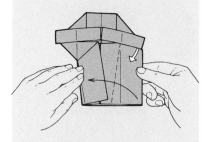

16 Repeat steps 14 and 15 with the right-hand side.

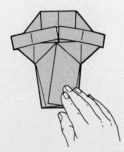

17 This should be the result. Press the paper flat.

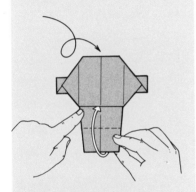

18 Turn the paper over. Valley fold the bottom edge up and tuck it . . .

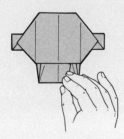

19 underneath the top layer of paper. Press the paper flat.

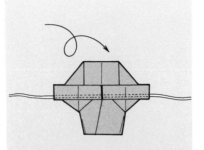

20 Turn the paper over. Place the piece of string underneath the middle flap of paper, so it protrudes equally from either side of the model.

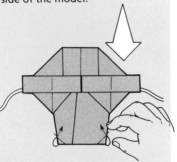

21 Inside reverse fold just a little of the bottom corners.

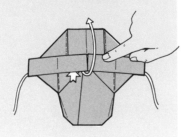

22 Lift the top section of paper upright, so the shoe's back becomes three-dimensional.

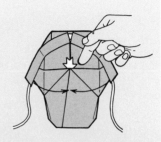

23 Insert your forefinger inside the bottom section of paper and open it out slightly, thereby shaping the shoe's toe.

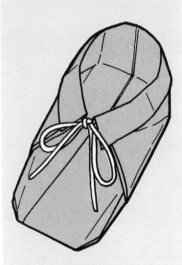

24 To complete the baby's shoe, tie the string into a bow. The actual tying of the bow will hold the model together. Now have a go at making a pair of shoes.

PIG BASE (Traditional)

In origami a base is a folded shape that does not resemble anything special, but it can be used to make many different models. Not all origami models start with a base because, as you have already discovered, a few folded shapes are also used. Each base is named after the best-known model for which it is used. Let us start with the simplest of bases, the pig base. The pig base is a development of the cupboard fold. Use a square of paper, white side up.

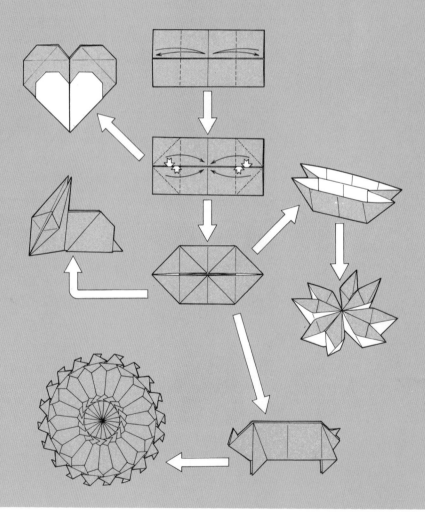

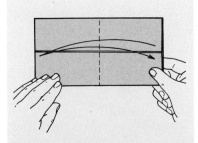

1 Begin with a cupboard fold (see page 16). Valley fold it in half from side to side. Press it flat and unfold it.

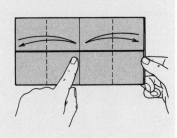

2 Valley fold the sides over to meet the middle fold-line. Press them flat and unfold them.

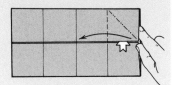

3 Insert your forefinger between the upper right-hand layers of paper as shown, and . . .

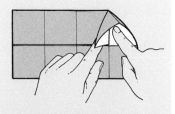

4 pull the top layer over towards the left, along the valley fold-line made in step 2.

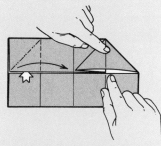

5 Press the paper down neatly into the shape of a triangle. Insert your forefinger between the upper left-hand layers of paper and . . .

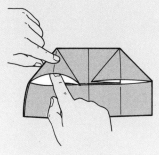

6 pull the top layer over towards the right, along the valley fold-line made in step 2. Press the paper down neatly into the shape of a triangle.

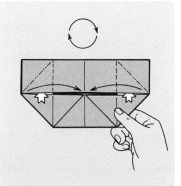

7 Turn the paper around. Repeat steps 3 to 6.

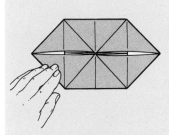

8 Press the paper flat, thereby completing the pig base. Very few models have been made from this base, but we do hope you find the following ones interesting.

W-BOAT/FLOWER *(Traditional)*

By uniting two similar models it is possible (as in the flower) to create a different kind of model.

Use a square of paper, white side up.

W-BOAT

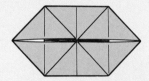

1 Begin with a pig base (see page 29). Turn it over.

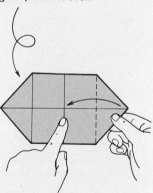

2 Valley fold the right-hand point into the middle. In doing so, . . .

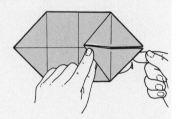

3 let the two points from underneath flick around.

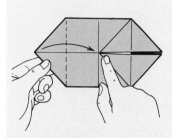

4 Repeat steps 2 and 3 with the left-hand point.

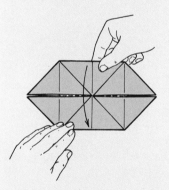

5 Valley fold the paper in half from top to bottom.

6 Press the paper flat, thereby completing the W-boat.

FLOWER

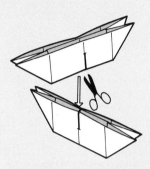

7 Use two squares of paper, identical in size. Fold each square into a W-boat, with the coloured side face up in step 1 of the pig base (see page 29). Cut along the middle fold-line of one boat, from the bottom edge to the middle. With the remaining boat, cut from the top edge to the middle. Slot both boats together.

8 Open out the eight triangular points and shape them into petals, thereby completing the flower.

PIG *(Traditional)*

This is the model which has given its name to this particular base.
Take your time in making the reverse folds on the head and tail.

Use a square of paper, white side up.

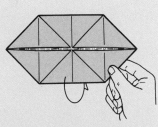

1 Begin with a pig base (see page 29). Mountain fold it in half from bottom to top.

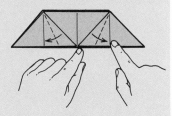

2 Valley fold the right-hand triangular point over so its sloping edge lies along the adjacent fold-line. Repeat with the left-hand triangular point, thereby . . .

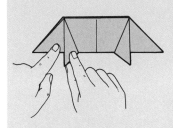

3 making two of the pig's legs.

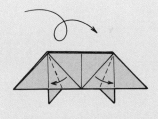

4 Turn the paper over. Repeat step 2.

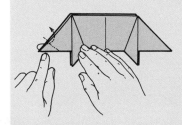

5 Inside reverse fold the left-hand point, thereby making the snout. This is what you do. . . .

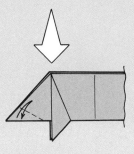

6 Fold and unfold the left-hand point as shown.

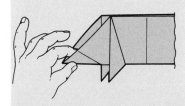

7 Pinch the point and . . .

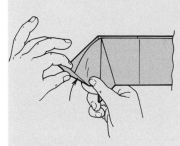

8 push it up inside the model along the fold-lines already made in step 6.

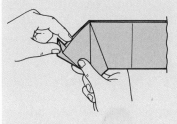

9 To complete the snout, press the paper flat.

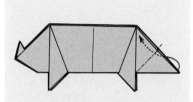

10 Inside reverse fold the right-hand point, thereby making the tail. Just like before, . . .

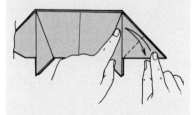

11 fold and unfold the right-hand point as shown.

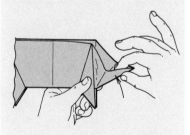

12 Pinch the point and push it up inside the model along the fold-lines made in step 11.

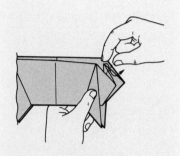

13 To complete the tail, make another inside reverse fold so the point's tip protrudes slightly.

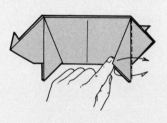

14 Valley fold the rear leg over to the right along its vertical edge. Repeat behind.

15 Here is the completed pig.

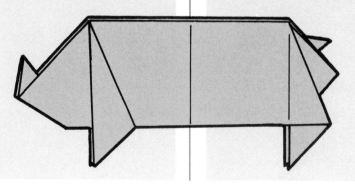

FLOWER *(Fumie Ono)*

To create this beautiful piece of origami the creator has folded 20 traditional pigs which she has then glued together to form a much more complex design. With this style of folding the right choice of paper will help, more often than not, to enhance the finished product.

Use 20 squares of paper, identical in size. You will also need a tube of paper glue.

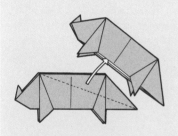

1 Begin by folding each of the squares into a completed step 9 of the traditional pig (see page 31). Slot one model inside another on a line between the tip of the right-hand point and the top of the front leg. Glue them together.

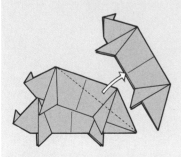

2 Carefully keep on slotting and gluing the remaining models together . . .

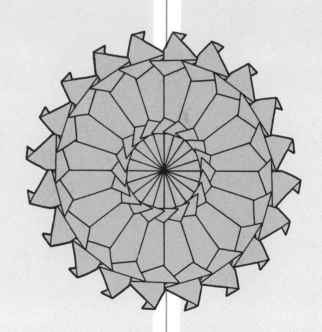

3 until you have built up this flower design. By using 15 models you can create a dish.

RABBIT *(Steve Biddle)*

Action origami folds are very popular. This particular action model is based upon the traditional Japanese rabbit; I have just created the back legs and ear-wagging mechanism.

Use a square of paper, white side up.

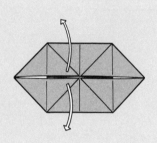

1 Begin with a pig base (see page 29). Pinch the left-hand triangular points and . . .

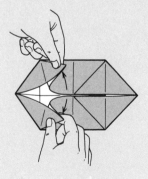

2 stretch them apart, . . .

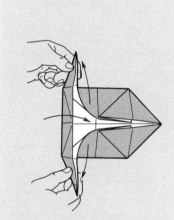

3 thereby taking the left-hand side point into the middle, at the same time . . .

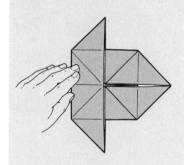

4 flattening it out.

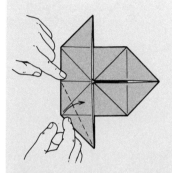

5 Narrow down the bottom left-hand point by valley folding it over on a line between its tip and the middle of the left-hand side.

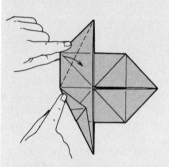

6 Repeat step 5 with the top left-hand point, . . .

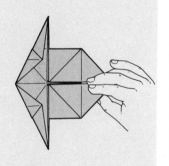

7 thereby making the ears.

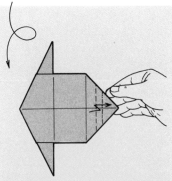

8 Turn the paper over. Step fold the right-hand side point. This is what you do. . . .

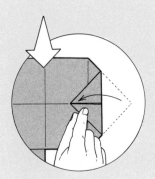

9 Valley fold the point over towards the left. Press it flat.

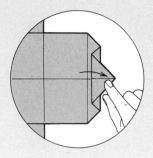

10 To complete, valley fold the point back out towards the right, thereby making a small pleat in the paper.

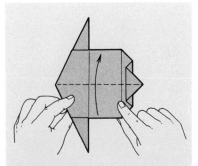

11 Valley fold the paper in half from bottom to top.

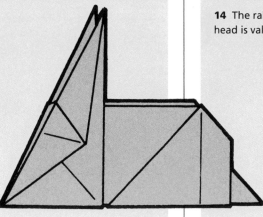

12 Here is the completed rabbit.

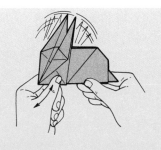

13 To make the rabbit waggle its ears, hold it as shown and, from the bottom, pull upon the head section's topmost layer of paper.

14 The rabbit will stand up if its head is valley folded to one side.

DOUBLE HEART (Steve Biddle)

This model has been created around the crease pattern of half a pig base. Just fold very carefully and everything will fall easily into place.

Use a square of paper, white side up.

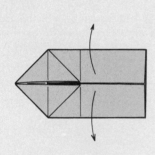

1 Begin by folding half a pig base (see page 29) on the square's left-hand side. Unfold it completely.

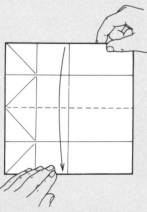

2 Valley fold the paper in half from top to bottom, with the white side on top.

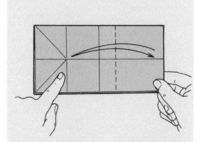

3 Valley fold the right-hand side over to where the diagonal, vertical and horizontal fold-lines intersect. Press it flat, then unfold it.

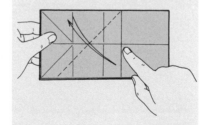

4 Valley fold the top edge down to lie along the left-hand side of the fold-line made in step 3. Press it flat and unfold it.

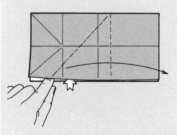

5 Insert your forefinger between the left-hand layers of paper and . . .

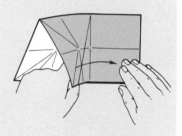

6 pull the top layer over to the right, along the valley fold-line made in step 3.

7 With your free hand, press the paper down neatly into the shape of a triangular roof.

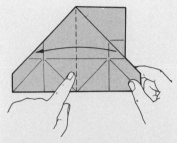

8 Valley fold the triangular roof in half from right to left.

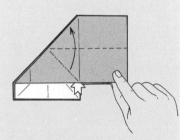

9 The following folds all take place along existing fold-lines. Valley fold the top layer of paper in half from bottom to top, while at the same time . . .

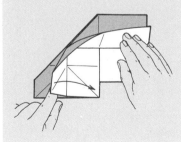

10 valley folding the top left-hand layer of paper in half from left to right.

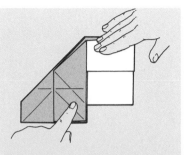

11 This should be the result. Press the paper flat.

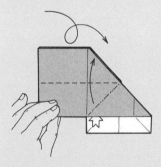

12 Turn the paper over. Repeat steps 9 to 11, thereby valley folding the right-hand layer in half from right to left.

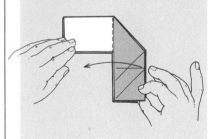

13 Valley fold the right-hand layer of paper over towards the left, as if turning over the page of a book.

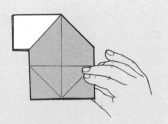

14 This should be the result. Press the paper flat.

15 Turn the paper over. Valley fold the top section of paper over, so it stands up in the air.

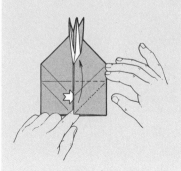

16 Along the existing fold-lines, reform the . . .

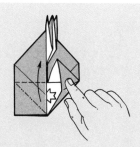

17 half pig base.

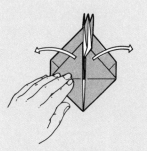

18 Pinch the triangular points and . . .

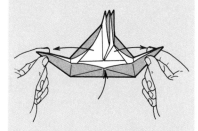

19 stretch them apart, thereby flattening out the bottom point, at the same time taking it . . .

20 underneath the upright section of paper.

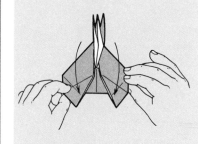

21 Valley fold the triangular points down, thereby returning the paper to a 'flat' position.

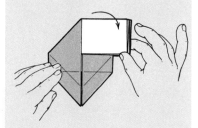

22 Valley fold the upright section of paper down and over to the right.

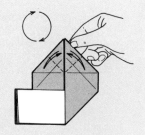

23 Turn the paper around. Valley fold the top triangular points in half as shown. Press them flat and unfold them.

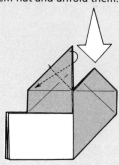

24 Inside reverse fold the triangular points along the fold-lines made in step 23.

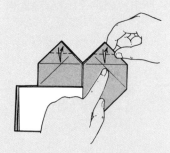

25 Valley fold the top points in half from top to bottom. Press them flat and unfold them.

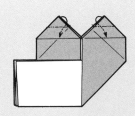

26 Inside reverse fold the top points along the fold-lines made in step 25.

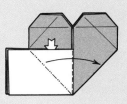

27 Valley fold the bottom section of paper over, so it stands up in the air.

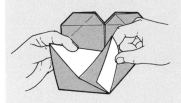

28 From the top open out the upright section of paper and . . .

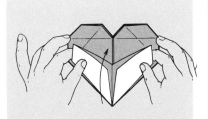

29 squash it down neatly . . .

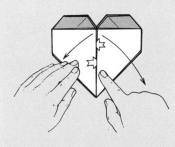

30 into a rectangular heart shape. Reach inside the top layer of paper and . . .

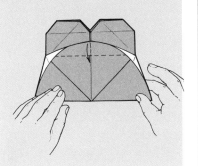

31 very gently open it out into . . .

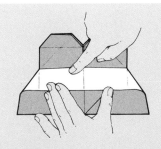

32 the shape of a house. Press the paper flat.

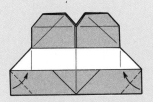

33 Valley fold the bottom corners up to meet the adjacent horizontal edge.

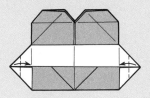

34 Valley fold the side points over to meet their adjacent vertical fold-line.

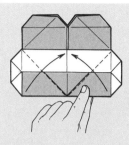

35 Valley fold the right- and left-hand halves of the bottom edge up . . .

36 to meet the middle fold-line. Press the paper flat.

37 Turn the paper over. Valley fold the top layer of paper in half from right to left.

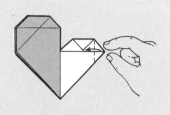

38 Valley fold the right-hand side point over towards the left, thereby making a vertical edge.

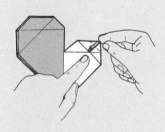

39 Valley fold the top right-hand point down, thereby making a sloping edge.

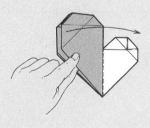

40 Valley fold two left-hand layers of paper over to the right.

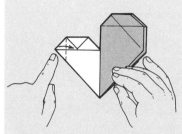

41 Valley fold the left-hand side point over towards the right, thereby making a vertical edge.

42 Repeat step 36 with the top left-hand point. Valley fold the right-hand layer of paper over to the left.

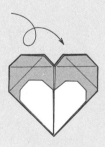

43 Turn the paper over, thereby completing the double heart.

WINDMILL BASE
(Traditional)

This base is very useful when making decorative forms of origami. Once the windmill base's four triangular flaps have been squashed into a multiple of four preliminary folds (see page 123), it can be used to make a much more complex piece of origami, such as the crab on pages 187–191. The windmill base is a development of the pig base. To make the windmill base, use a square of paper, white side up, and follow the instructions overleaf.

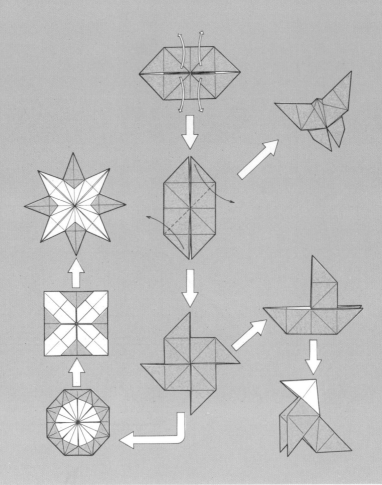

WINDMILL BASE

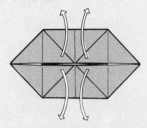

1 Begin with a pig base (see page 29). The right- and left-hand side points have to be flattened out. The easy way to do this is to . . .

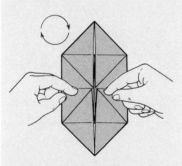

2 turn the paper around so it is lengthways on. Pinch the bottom triangular points and . . .

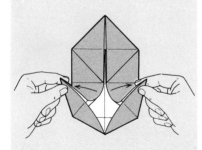

3 stretch them apart, . . .

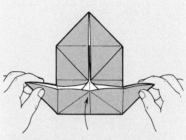

4 thereby taking the bottom point into the middle, at the same time . . .

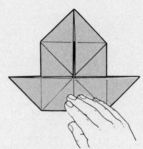

5 flattening it out.

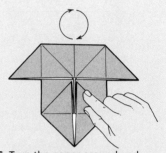

6 Turn the paper around and repeat step 2.

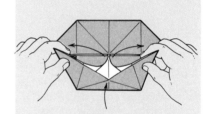

7 Repeat steps 3 to 5.

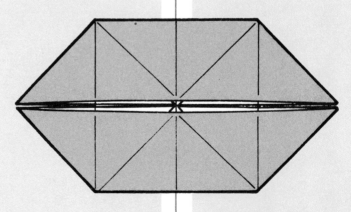

8 Here is the completed windmill base.

WINDMILL BASE TOYS
(Traditional)

The windmill base can be folded into many simple models, of which the following two are the most popular. The trick of the magic boat has its origins in Japan. On the other hand, the pajarita (Spanish for 'little bird') is thought to have originated in Spain, but it is also known in Germany as a crow and in Great Britain it used to be called a hobby horse. In Spain and France, the pajarita is recognized as a symbol of childhood.

Use a square of paper, white side up.

MAGIC BOAT

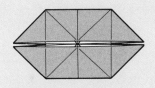

1 Begin with a windmill base (see opposite).

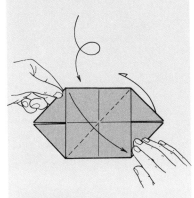

2 Turn the base over. Valley fold it in half from top left to bottom right, thereby letting . . .

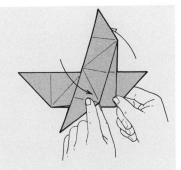

3 the triangular points swing into this position.

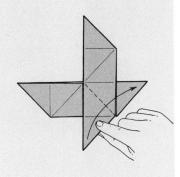

4 Valley fold the bottom triangular point up and across to the right.

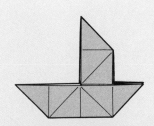

5 Here is the completed magic boat. The trick, and it is best performed for a very young child, is to ask how the boat can change its direction when he or she is holding the bow.

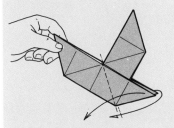

6 Ask him to hold the bow of the boat and shut his eyes. Valley fold over the stern triangular points, so that now he appears to be holding the mast instead of the bow.

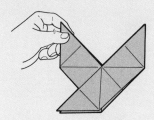

7 He will open his eyes in order to prove you wrong, only to find out that you are right. Tell him how the trick works and give him the magic boat as a gift.

PAJARITA

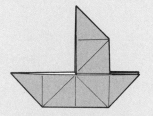

8 Begin with a completed step 4.

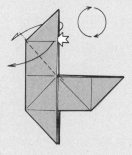

9 Turn the paper around. Outside reverse fold the top triangular point. This is what you do. . . .

10 Open out the model a little, thereby separating the top point's two layers of paper.

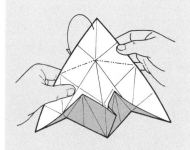

11 Press down on the fold-lines as shown, thereby converting them into mountain folds, at the same time . . .

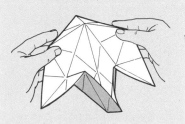

12 taking the top point behind.

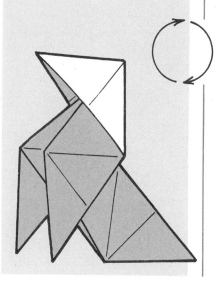

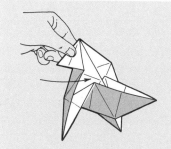

13 Gently arrange the layers of paper back . . .

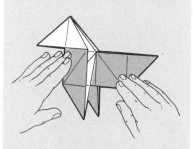

14 into this position. Press the paper flat.

15 Turn the paper around, thereby completing the pajarita.

BUTTERFLY (*Traditional*)

This elegantly simple Japanese fold is developed from the windmill base.

Use a square of paper, white side up.

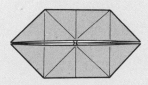

1 Begin with a windmill base (see page 42).

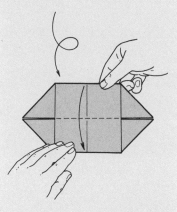

2 Turn the base over. Valley fold it in half from top to bottom.

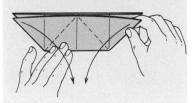

3 Valley fold the top right- and left-hand triangular points downwards.

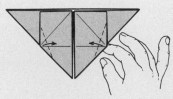

4 Valley fold a little of the right- and left-hand side points in and on a slant.

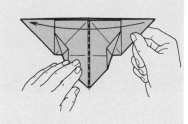

5 Valley fold the paper in half from right to left.

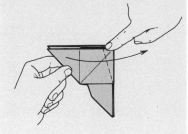

6 Valley fold the left-hand top layer of paper over on a slant to the right.

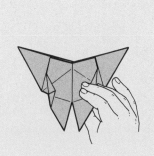

7 Press the paper flat.

8 Turn the paper over. Valley fold the middle point over, so it stands up in the air.

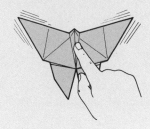

9 Here is the completed butterfly. If you gently press upon the upright point the butterfly will flutter its wings.

PENDANT *(Traditional)*

The following windmill base decorations (pendant, stars and mosaic) are only a few of the many that can be made.

Use a square of paper, white side up.

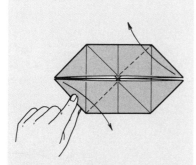

1 Begin with a windmill base (see page 42). Valley fold the top right-hand triangular point up and the bottom left-hand triangular point down, thereby . . .

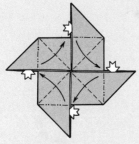

2 making the traditional windmill from which the windmill base has obtained its name. Open out and squash the four triangular points down neatly, so they meet in the middle and make four small squares. Press the paper flat.

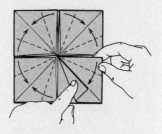

3 Valley fold the inner two edges of each small square over, so they lie along their respective square's middle fold-line.

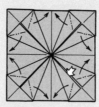

4 Open out the inner edge of one small square and . . .

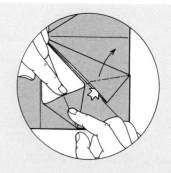

5 squash it down neatly. Press the paper flat. Repeat with the opposite edge. Repeat steps 4 and 5 with all the other small squares.

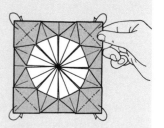

6 Mountain fold the four corners behind on a line that joins the tops of their respective inner edges, thereby making little triangles on the reverse side. Press the paper flat.

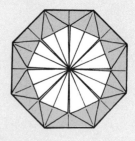

7 Here is the completed pendant.

STARS *(Traditional)*

This model is a good lesson in the very important origami technique of petal folding.

Use a square of paper, white side up.

FOUR-POINTED STAR

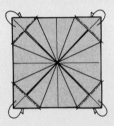

1 Begin with a completed step 3 of the pendant (see opposite). Now repeat step 6 of the same model.

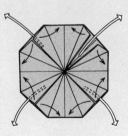

2 Here is the origami technique known as a petal fold.

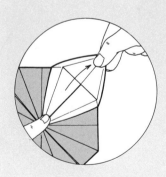

3 Unfold the inner edges of one small square. Pinch and lift up its front flap of paper.

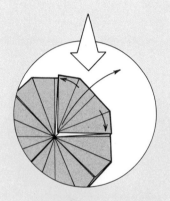

4 Continue to lift up the flap, so . . .

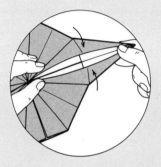

5 its edges meet in the middle. Press the paper flat, thereby making it diamond-shaped and completing the petal fold.

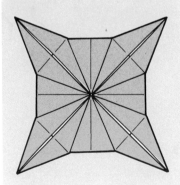

6 Repeat steps 3 to 5 with the other small squares. Press the paper flat, thereby completing the four-pointed star.

EIGHT-POINTED STAR

7 Use two squares of paper, identical in size. Fold each square into a four-pointed star. Place the two stars crosswise and back to back. Lock them together by wrapping the four little triangles made in step 1 around the other star.

8 Here is the completed eight-pointed star.

MOSAIC DECORATION
(Traditional)

When carefully folded out of colourful paper, this decoration looks perfect glued on to a gift box, or even used as a drinks' place mat. You could also try folding many mosaics and then building up your own unique patterns.

Use a square of paper, coloured side up.

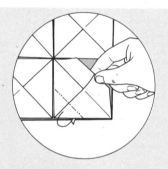

1 Begin with the square's coloured side on top and fold a completed step 2 of the pendant (see page 46). Valley fold the front flap of each small square in half from the middle to the corners.

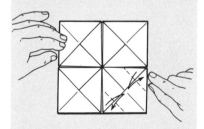

2 Valley fold one small square's side points into its middle. Press them flat and unfold them.

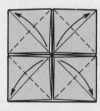

3 Mountain fold the side points along the fold-lines made in step 2, thereby tucking them underneath the small square. Repeat steps 2 and 3 with the other small squares.

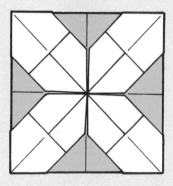

4 Here is the completed mosaic decoration.

DIAPER FOLD
(Traditional)

S o far we have made folds and bases from a square's vertical and horizontal axes. Let us now turn the square around so it looks like a diamond, and use its diagonal axis, thereby developing a whole new range of folds and bases.

When a square of paper is folded in half along its diagonal, or you have to make a fold in such a way, it is described as a 'diaper' fold – an American term which is now used internationally. In Japan, it is called a shawl or triangle fold.

To make a diaper fold, use a square of paper, white side up, and follow the instructions overleaf.

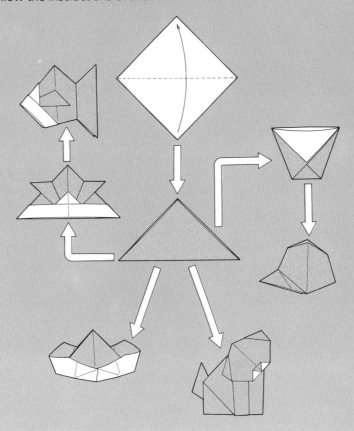

DIAPER FOLD

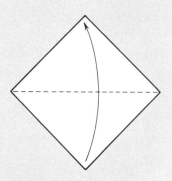

1 Turn the square around to look like a diamond, with the white side uppermost. Valley fold it in half from bottom to top, thereby making . . .

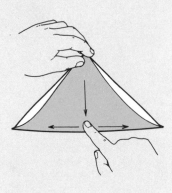

2 a triangle. To complete the diaper fold, press it flat along its bottom edge.

CUP *(Traditional)*

If made from a square of plain waxed paper, this very practical piece of origami can be used as an instant drinking cup.

Use a square of paper, white side up.

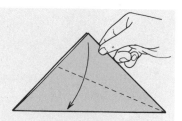

1 Begin with a diaper fold (see left). From the bottom right-hand corner, valley fold the top layer of paper down to meet the bottom edge, but do not press the paper completely flat. Instead . . .

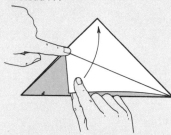

2 press it only a little, at the left-hand side. Return the layer of paper to its original position.

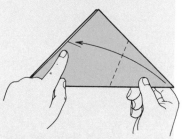

3 Valley fold the bottom right-hand point over to meet the fold mark that was made in step 2.

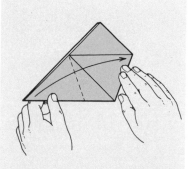

4 Valley fold the bottom left-hand point over to meet the opposite side.

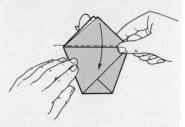

5 Valley fold the top point down. Repeat behind.

6 Slightly open the paper out along the top edge. This completes the cup.

CAP *(Traditional)*

A creative technique in origami is to use a completed model as the starting point when making another one. This cap has been developed from the traditional cup shape.

Use a square of paper, white side up.

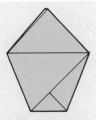

1 Begin with a completed step 4 of the cup (see opposite).

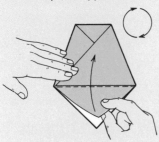

2 Turn the paper around. Valley fold the bottom point up along the horizontal edge. Later on, this point will become the peak of your cap.

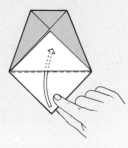

3 Insert the remaining bottom point up and inside the model. Press the paper flat.

4 Valley fold the peak down, thereby making a pleat in the paper.

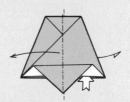

5 The cap now has to be opened out and have its top pushed in. This is what to do. . . .

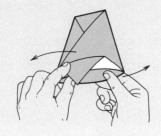

6 Turn the cap sideways on and open the paper along the bottom edge. As you do so, . . .

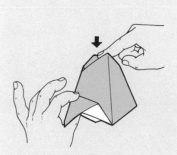

7 push in the top of the cap. Press the paper flat.

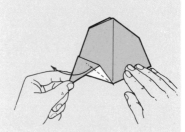

8 Hold the peak and . . .

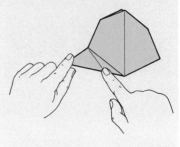

9 pull it upwards, pressing it into place as shown. This completes the cap.

SOMBRERO *(Traditional)*

Try to make this model look as true to life as possible by rolling its brim over during the final stages of folding.

Use a square of paper, white side up.

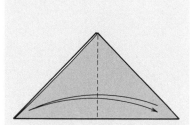

1 Begin with a diaper fold (see page 50). Valley fold it in half from side to side. Press it flat and unfold it.

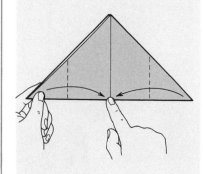

2 Valley fold the bottom points over to meet the middle of the bottom edge.

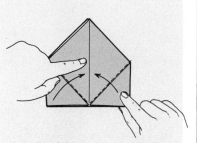

3 Valley fold the right- and left-hand halves of the bottom edge up to meet the middle fold-line.

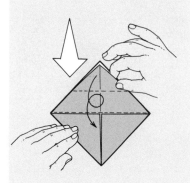

4 Valley fold the top point down into the middle and then . . .

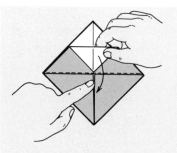

5 over along the middle.

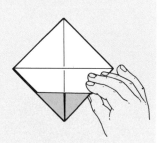

6 This should be the result. Press the paper flat.

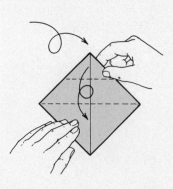

7 Turn the paper over. Repeat steps 4 and 5.

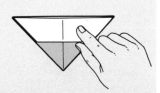

8 This should be the result. Press the paper flat.

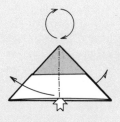

9 Turn the paper around. Open the paper along the bottom edge and . . .

10 collapse it . . .

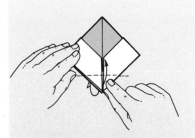

11 into this shape. Valley fold the bottom point up into the middle. Repeat behind.

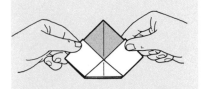

12 On either side of the model, pinch the outer layers of paper and . . .

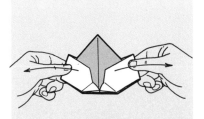

13 pull them apart . . .

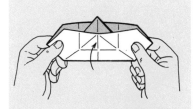

14 to make a flat sombrero.

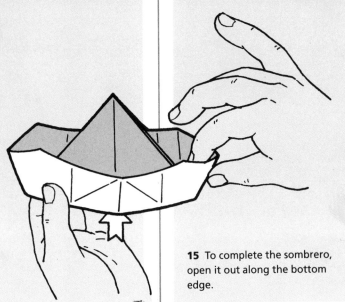

15 To complete the sombrero, open it out along the bottom edge.

PUPPY *(Steve Biddle)*

Try changing the angle of the head, nose and tail each time you make this model to see how many different expressions you can give your puppy. Why not create a different breed of puppy?

Use a square of paper, white side up.

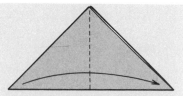

1 Begin with a diaper fold (see page 50). Valley fold it in half from left to right.

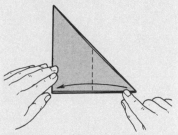

2 Valley fold the right-hand point over to meet the left-hand vertical edge, but do not press the paper completely flat. Instead . . .

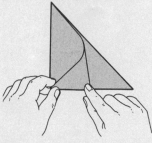

3 press it only a little, at the bottom point. Now take this fold mark over to meet . . .

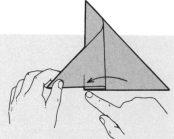

4 the vertical edge. Press the paper flat.

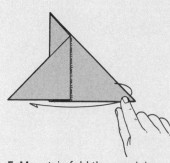

5 Mountain fold the remaining right-hand point behind, so it is symmetrical with the top one.

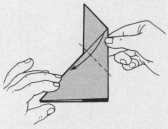

6 Valley fold the top point down and over towards the left, so the top of the right-hand vertical edge comes to rest somewhere along the sloping edge.

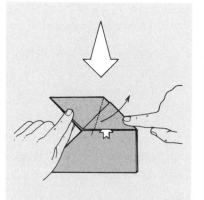

7 Open out the point . . .

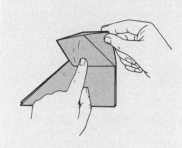

8 and squash it . . .

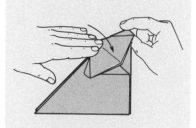

9 down neatly, thereby making the start of the puppy's face.

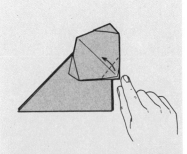

10 Valley fold the topmost bottom point of the puppy's face up, thereby making a small white triangle.

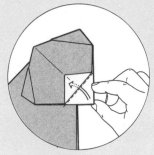

11 Tuck the remaining bottom point underneath the white triangle.

12 Valley fold the white triangle in half from top to bottom, to make the puppy's nose.

13 Valley fold the right-hand layer of paper over towards the left on a slant, to suggest the puppy's front paw.

14 Valley fold the left-hand point over to meet the puppy's front paw.

15 Valley fold the remaining left-hand point up and over, to suggest the puppy's tail. Press the paper flat.

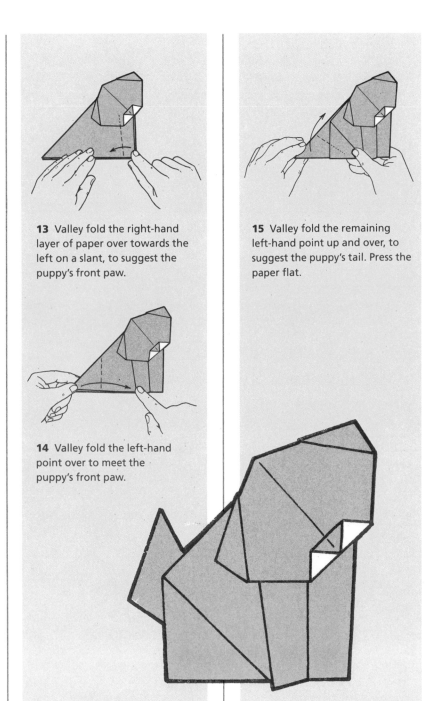

16 Here is the completed puppy.

KABUTO *(Traditional)*

Many of the traditional Japanese origami models have a symbolic meaning. This fold is no exception, as it symbolizes bravery. It is usually folded by many Japanese children on 5 May, a date which is celebrated throughout Japan as children's day.

Use a square of paper, white side up.

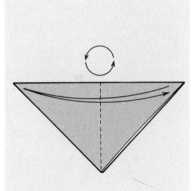

1 Begin with a diaper fold (see page 50). Turn the diaper fold around so it points towards you. Valley fold it in half from side to side. Press it flat and unfold it.

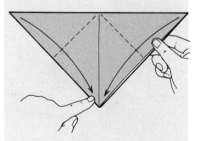

2 Valley fold the right- and left-hand halves of the top edge down to meet the middle fold-line.

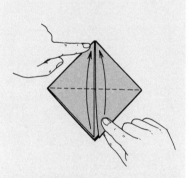

3 Valley fold the two bottom points up to meet the top point.

4 Valley fold the points out from the middle as shown.

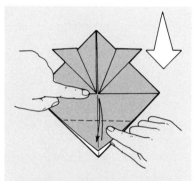

5 Valley fold the bottom point up into the middle. Press it flat and unfold it.

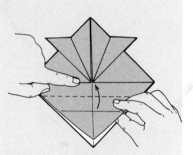

6 Valley fold the bottom point up so the fold-line made in step 5 lies along the middle.

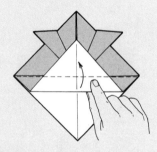

7 Valley fold the horizontal edge up and over along the middle.

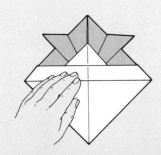

8 This should be the result. Press the paper flat.

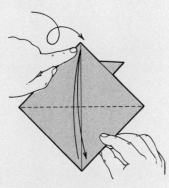

9 Turn the paper over. Valley fold it in half from bottom to top. Press it flat and unfold it.

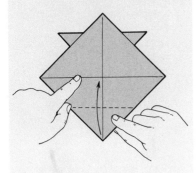

10 Valley fold the bottom point up into the middle.

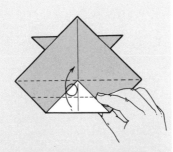

11 Valley fold the bottom edge up into the middle and then over . . .

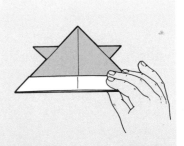

12 along the middle.

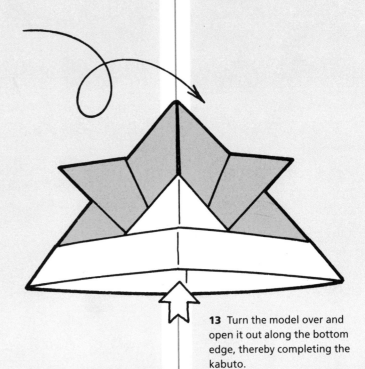

13 Turn the model over and open it out along the bottom edge, thereby completing the kabuto.

KIRIKOMI ORIGAMI
(Paper cutting)

Many paperfolders feel that it is wrong to cut the paper in any way: they believe that any changes to the paper should be made only by folding it. They will often fold with great complexity to make a model that could be made more easily if it incorporated a cut or two. Originally in Japan it was acceptable (and still is among some paperfolders) to make an incision in the paper, and it was not until origami became popular in the West that the 'no cutting' rule was applied. Maybe, like us, you feel that an incision or two is acceptable because the original square or rectangle of paper is not really being destroyed.

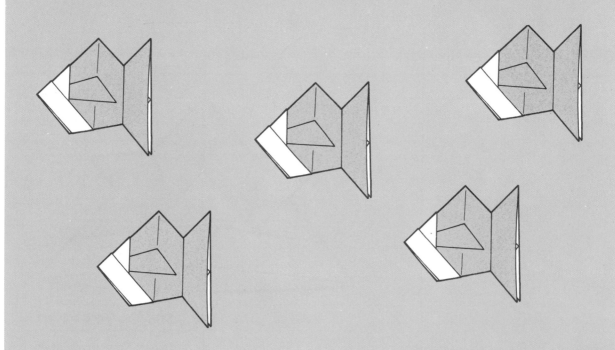

GOLDFISH *(Traditional)*

This goldfish is a perfect example of kirikomi. Its foundation is the traditional kabuto. As with any origami model you can vary the angles of the folds to make your very own model, but always remember to give credit to the original creator of your model, if there is one.

Use a square of paper, white side up.

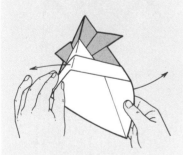

1 Begin with a completed step 8 of the kabuto (see page 57). The model now has to be opened out. This is what you do. . . .

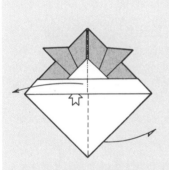

2 Turn the paper sideways on, then take hold of the middle layers of paper and the bottom point. Carefully pull them apart, so . . .

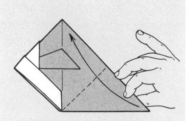

3 the paper collapses into this shape. Press the paper flat. Valley fold the bottom right-hand point up to meet the top point.

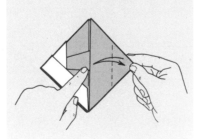

4 Valley fold the right-hand side point into the middle. Press it flat and unfold it.

5 Return the bottom right-hand point to its original position.

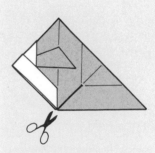

6 Cut the top layer of paper along the fold-line as shown. Repeat behind.

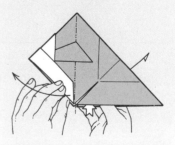

7 Open the paper out, so it collapses . . .

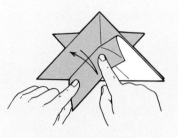

8 into this shape. Valley fold the paper in half from bottom to top.

9 Valley fold the right-hand sloping edge down and towards the opposite side on a line between the middle and the point where the cut ends. Do not press the paper flat. Instead, . . .

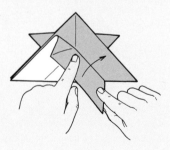

10 press the paper only from the bottom edge to the middle. Return the edge to its original position.

11 Repeat steps 9 and 10 with the left-hand sloping edge.

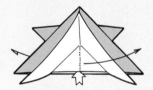

12 Open the paper along the bottom edge. Carefully pull . . .

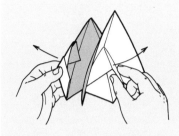

13 the paper apart, so the goldfish's tail starts to fold itself along the fold-lines made in steps 9 to 11.

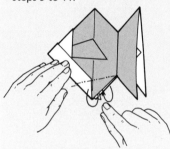

14 Press the paper flat into this shape. Shape the goldfish's tummy with a mountain fold. Repeat behind.

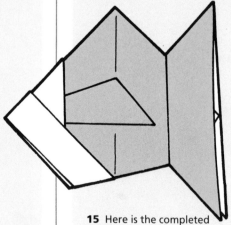

15 Here is the completed goldfish.

KITE AND
DIAMOND BASES
(Traditional)

The kite base is named for its shape. During the folding of this base, as with any other, you should make your folds accurately. The diamond base uses the kite base as its foundation. Like the kite base, this one is also named for its shape.

To make either of these bases, use a square of paper, white side up, and follow the instructions overleaf.

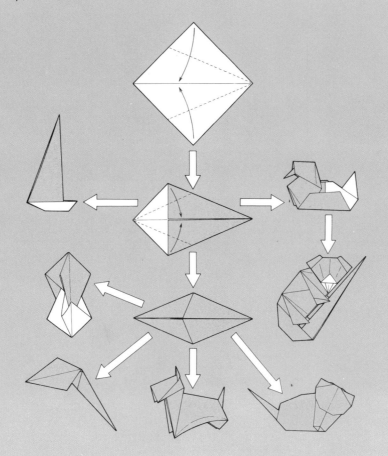

KITE BASE

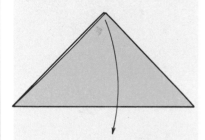

1 Begin with a diaper fold (see page 50). Unfold it completely.

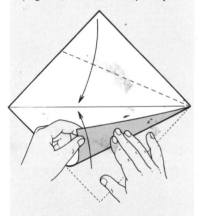

2 From the right-hand corner, valley fold the top and bottom sloping edges to meet the middle fold-line. Press them flat.

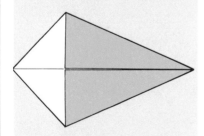

3 Here is the completed kite base.

DIAMOND BASE

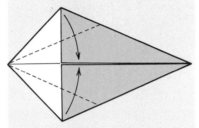

1 Begin with a kite base (see left). From the left-hand corner, valley fold the top . . .

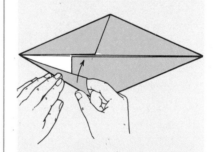

2 and bottom sloping edges to meet the middle fold-line. Press them flat.

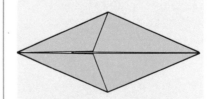

3 Here is the completed diamond base.

STALK AND LEAF
(Traditional)

This stalk and leaf is one of many models that can be folded from the diamond base. Using the techniques already learned, see what new leaves you can create.

Use a square of paper, white side up.

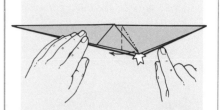

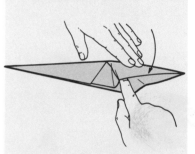

4 Squash fold the right-hand point, thereby creating a leaf, . . .

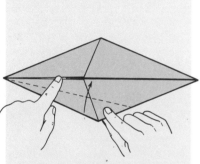

1 Begin with a diamond base (see opposite). From the left-hand corner, valley fold the bottom sloping edge up to meet the middle fold-line.

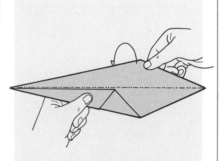

3 Mountain fold the paper in half from top to bottom.

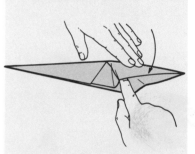

5 as shown here.

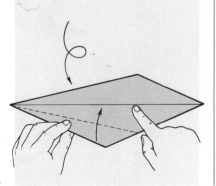

2 Turn the paper over. Once again from the left-hand corner, valley fold the bottom sloping edge up to meet the middle fold-line.

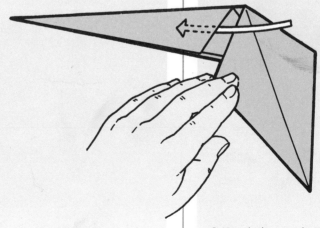

6 Here is the completed stalk and leaf. The stalk has a pocket, into which a flower can be inserted.

DECORATION *(Traditional)*

Many origami models make ideal Christmas tree decorations, but to look really beautiful they must be neatly folded.

Use two squares of paper, identical in size.

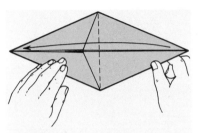

1 Begin by folding one of the squares into a diamond base (see page 62). Valley fold it in half from right to left, thereby . . .

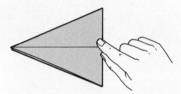

2 making a triangle.

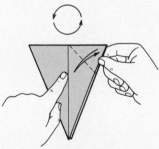

3 Turn the triangle around so it points towards you. Valley fold the right-hand half of the top edge down to meet the middle fold-line. Press it flat, then unfold it .

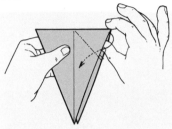

4 Inside reverse fold the right-hand half of the top edge along the fold-lines made in step 3.

5 This shows the reverse fold taking place. Repeat steps 3 and 4 with the left-hand half of the top edge.

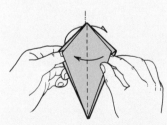

6 Arrange the model so it becomes three-dimensional, thereby making one half of the decoration. Repeat steps 1 to 6 with the remaining square.

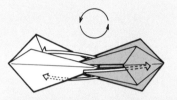

7 The two halves of the decoration have been turned around on to their sides and are shown here being locked together. The points of one half must be inserted into the pockets of the other half, and vice versa. This is easier if the pockets are opened out slightly first.

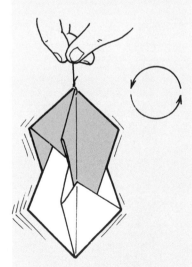

8 Turn the locked halves around, thereby completing the decoration. To hang up the decoration, thread a length of cotton through the top.

YACHT *(Traditional)*

When folding this model, watch out for the origami technique of making a rabbit ear.

Use a square of paper, white side up.

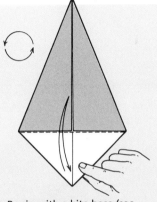

1 Begin with a kite base (see page 62). Turn it around as shown. Valley fold the smaller triangle up and along the base of the larger one. Press it flat and unfold it.

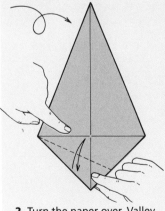

2 Turn the paper over. Valley fold the bottom left-hand sloping edge up to meet the fold-line made in step 1. Press it flat and unfold it. Repeat with the bottom right-hand sloping edge, but do not unfold it.

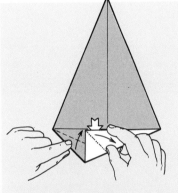

3 Here is the rabbit ear. This is what you do. . . .

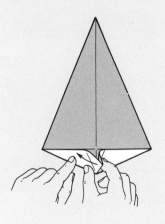

4 Pinch together the sloping edges along the fold-lines made in step 2. Fold the small triangular flap that appears . . .

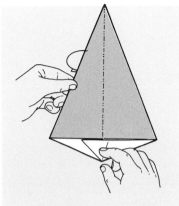

5 to one side and press it flat, thereby completing the rabbit ear. Mountain fold the paper in half from side to side.

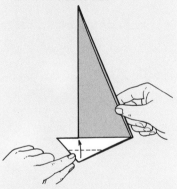

6 Shape the hull with a valley fold.

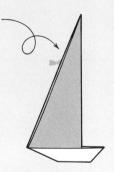

7 Turn the model over to complete the yacht.

WILD DUCK *(Traditional)*

You should find the following model helpful for understanding inside and outside reverse folds.

Use a square of paper, white side up.

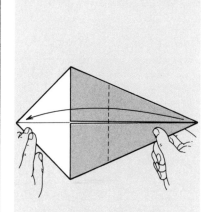

1 Begin with a kite base (see page 62). Valley fold it in half from right to left.

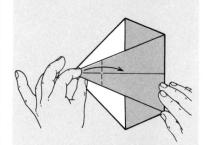

2 Valley fold the left-hand point over to where the vertical edge and the horizontal fold-line intersect.

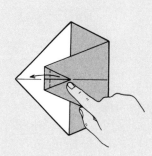

3 Valley fold the point back out towards the left, thereby making a small pleat in the paper.

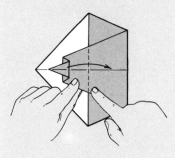

4 Valley fold what remains of the point over towards the right on a line between the top and bottom points.

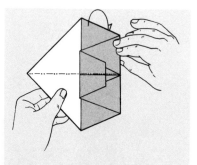

5 Mountain fold the paper in half from top to bottom.

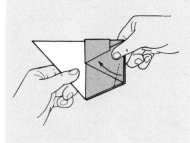

6 Pull the duck's chest up and press it flat into the position shown in step 7.

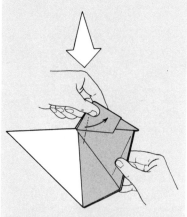

7 Pull the head up and press it flat into the position shown in step 8.

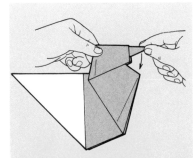

8 Pull the beak down. (By pleating the paper in steps 1 to 5, a nasty series of outside and inside reverse folds has been eliminated. This technique can be used on most, but not all, reverse folds.)

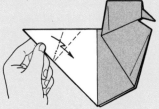

9 Step fold the duck's tail as shown.

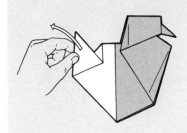

10 Press the tail flat, then unfold it.

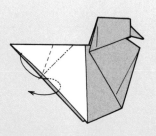

11 Using the fold-lines made in steps 9 and 10 as a guide, inside reverse fold the tail . . .

12 into the model and reverse fold it back out.

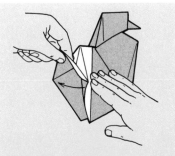

13 Press the paper flat.

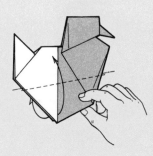

14 Valley fold the bottom point up, thereby making a wing. Repeat behind.

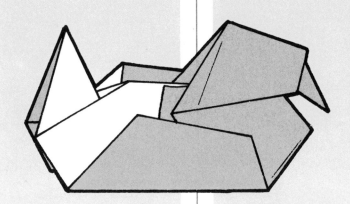

15 Here is the completed wild duck.

CAT (Steve Biddle)

If you use a few folds and just fold the main features, you can create a simple model that suggests a whole form, and this cat is a perfect example of that technique. As always, once you have learned how to fold this model you can make it your own by changing around the angle of the head, ears and tail.

Use a square of paper, white side up.

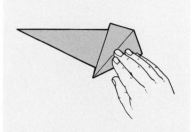

5 This should be the result.

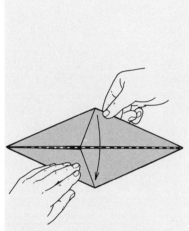

1 Begin with a diamond base (see page 62). Valley fold it in half from top to bottom.

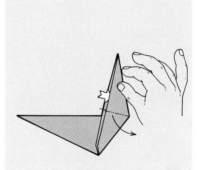

3 Open out the point and . . .

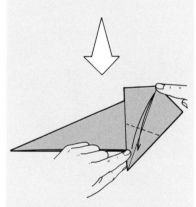

6 Valley fold the squashed point in half from bottom to top. Press it flat and unfold it.

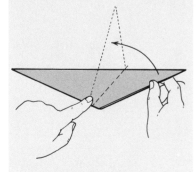

2 Valley fold the right-hand point into the position shown by the dotted lines.

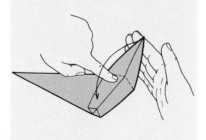

4 squash it down carefully and neatly towards you.

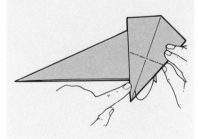

7 Mountain fold the point up inside the model along the fold-line made in step 6, to shape the cat's face.

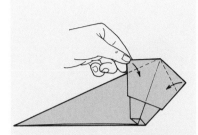

8 Valley fold the side points of the face inwards, to make the ears.

9 Shape the top of the head with a mountain fold.

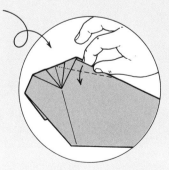

10 Turn the paper over. Shape the cat's back with a valley fold as shown.

11 This shows step 10 taking place. Note that the back of the head has been lifted up slightly so the valley fold can be made.

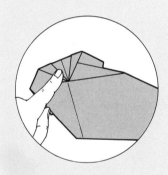

12 Press the paper flat.

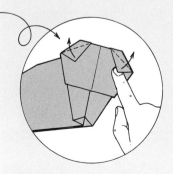

13 Turn the paper over. Shape the ears with valley folds.

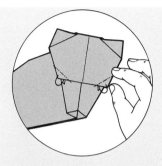

14 Round off the face with mountain folds.

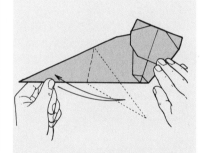

15 Valley fold the left-hand point into the position shown by the dotted lines. Press it flat and unfold it.

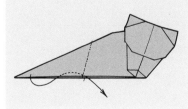

16 Using the fold-lines made in step 15 as a guide, . . .

17 inside reverse fold the point, to make the tail.

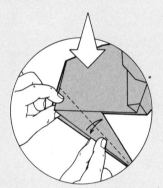

18 Starting from the tip, valley fold the tail's top layer in half. Press it flat and unfold it.

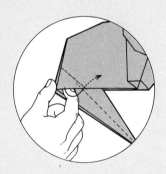

19 Once again starting from the tip, valley fold the top layer of the tail in half, at the same time . . .

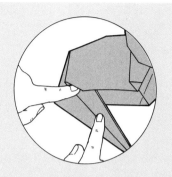

20 pushing the triangular area inwards as shown by the mountain fold-line in step 19.

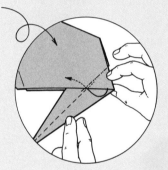

21 Turn the paper over. Repeat steps 18 to 20.

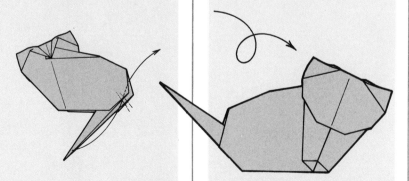

22 Reverse fold the tail outwards.

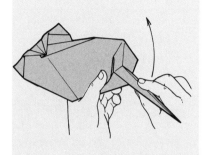

23 The reverse fold can easily be made if the back is opened out slightly.

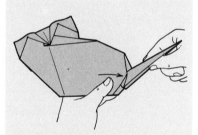

24 Press the paper flat, to complete the reverse fold.

25 Turn the model over. The cat is now complete.

SCOTTISH TERRIER
(Yasuhiro Sano)

Many paperfolders will fold just one theme, be it animals, birds or geometrical forms. Yasuhiro Sano has combined his love of dogs with that of origami to fold many breeds from the various folds and bases. In fact, his origami dogs are very much in demand by many admirers throughout the world. Yasuhiro Sano is the Chief Director of the Nippon Origami Association.

Use a square of paper, white side up.

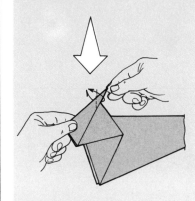

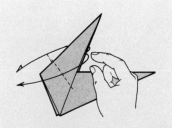

5 Outside reverse fold the point again so it points to the left.

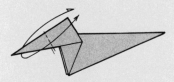

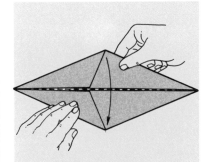

1 Begin with a diamond base (see page 62). Valley fold it in half from top to bottom.

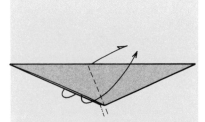

3 Outside reverse fold the left-hand point along the fold-lines made in step 2.

6 Once again, outside reverse fold the point, to make the terrier's muzzle.

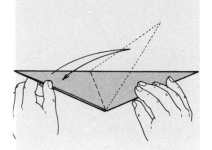

2 Valley fold the left-hand point into the position shown by the dotted lines. Press it flat and unfold it.

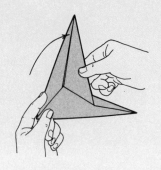

4 This shows the reverse fold taking place.

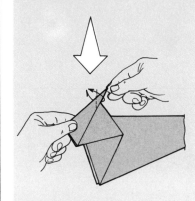

7 Finally, outside reverse fold the point's tip, thereby making the terrier's ears.

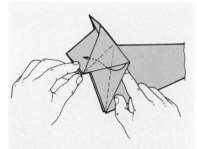

8 Valley fold the top layer of the neck in half, at the same time . . .

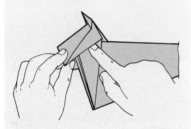

9 pushing the triangular area inwards as shown by the mountain fold-line in step 8.

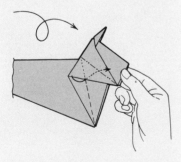

10 Turn the paper over. Repeat steps 8 and 9.

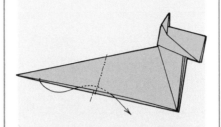

11 Inside reverse fold the left-hand point into the position shown in step 12.

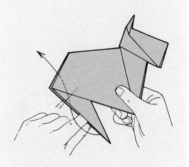

12 Reverse fold the point back out, to make the terrier's hind legs and tail.

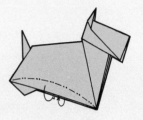

13 Mountain fold the bottom edge of paper inwards slightly.

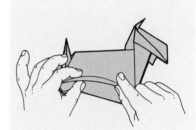

14 This shows step 13 taking place.

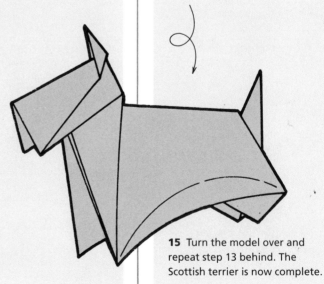

15 Turn the model over and repeat step 13 behind. The Scottish terrier is now complete.

KOALA (Kazuo Choshi)

Many paperfolders often fold with great complexity to create a combination theme from just one piece of paper. Although this style of folding can be very clever, it may be quite time-consuming, and the finished result can suffer from the many layers of paper that it contains. In most cases it is easier (and truer to life) to fold the various parts separately and then assemble them to make the model look more attractive and less bulky. Having said that, this koala is an exception to this rule, because the creator has folded a combination model using a simple and stylish technique.

Use a square of paper, coloured side up.

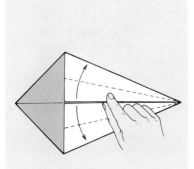

1 Begin with a kite base (see page 62). From the right-hand point, valley fold the middle edges out to meet their adjacent sloping edges, thereby . . .

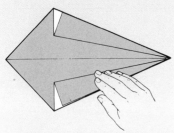

2 making a pleat on either side of the paper.

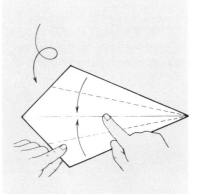

3 Turn the paper over. From the right-hand point, valley fold the top and bottom sloping edges over to meet the middle fold-line, as shown.

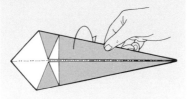

4 Mountain fold the paper in half from top to bottom.

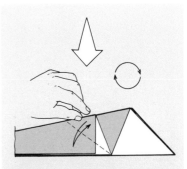

5 Turn the paper around. Valley fold the top layer of paper down to lie along the bottom edge. Press it flat and unfold it.

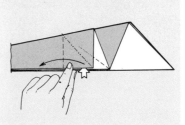

6 Open out the top layer of paper and . . .

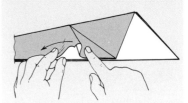

7 squash it down neatly, to make a triangular flap that points towards the left.

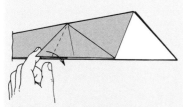

8 Valley fold the triangular flap over, so it points down. This is one of the koala's hind legs.

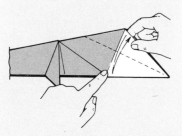

9 From the right-hand point, valley fold the top layer of paper down to lie along the bottom edge. Press it flat and unfold it.

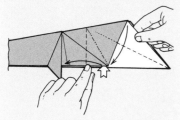

10 Repeat steps 6 and 7 with this layer of paper.

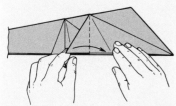

11 Valley fold the triangular flap that has just been made towards the right, as far as it will go.

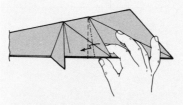

12 Step fold the triangular flap, to make one of the front legs.

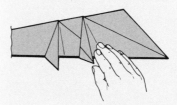

13 This should be the result. Repeat steps 5 to 12 behind.

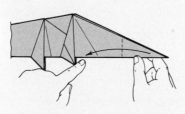

14 Valley fold the right-hand point over towards the left, so it comes to rest slightly short of the front leg.

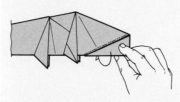

15 Mountain fold the point behind, along its sloping edge.

16 Valley fold the point around to the front using the 'behind' sloping edge as a guide to the position of the fold-line.

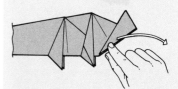

17 Unfold the point back to its original position.

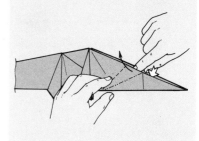

18 Using the fold-lines that have just been made, open out and squash the point down neatly into a diamond.

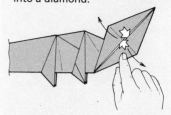

19 Reach inside and open out the layers of the squashed point, at the same time . . .

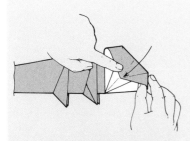

20 valley folding the opened layers in half from top to bottom, to make the koala's face and head.

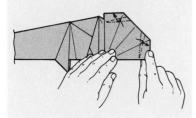

21 On either side of the head, make a step fold, to create the koala's ears.

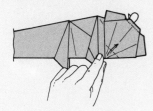

22 Shape the head with a mountain fold between the ears. Valley fold the bottom point up as shown, to make the nose.

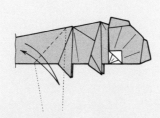

23 Valley fold the left-hand point into the position shown by the dotted lines. Press it flat and unfold it.

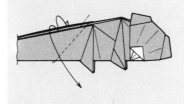

24 Outside reverse fold the left-hand point along the fold-lines made in step 23.

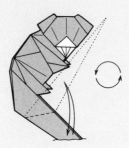

25 Turn the paper around. Valley fold the right-hand point into the position shown by the dotted lines. Press it flat and unfold it.

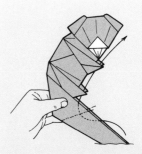

26 Inside reverse fold the right-hand point along the fold-lines made in step 25, to make a branch.

27 Release the koala's hind leg. Repeat behind. Shape the base of the branch with a mountain fold.

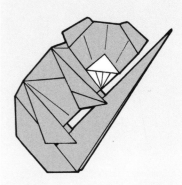

28 Here is the completed koala.

FISH BASE
(Traditional)

This is one of the best-known classic origami bases, the others being the frog and the bird bases. They all make a very good foundation from which to develop your own origami models. If you compare the crease pattern of an unfolded fish base with that of a kite base, you can see that it is really just a double kite base. To make a fish base, use a square of paper, white side up, and follow the instructions opposite.

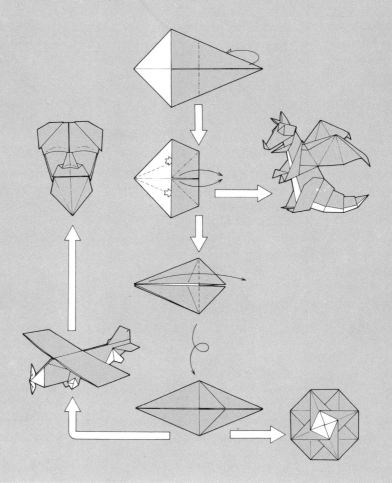

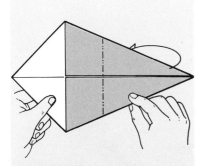

1 Begin with a kite base (see page 62). Mountain fold it in half from right to left.

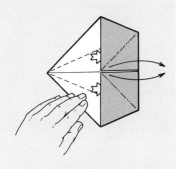

2 Pull the top flap of paper over . . .

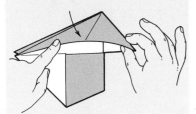

3 to the right, so its sloping edge comes to rest along the middle fold-line. Press the paper flat, to make a triangular pointed flap. Repeat steps 2 and 3 with the bottom flap of paper, to make . . .

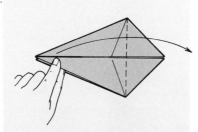

4 the fish base in its 'closed' form. Valley fold the left-hand point over to the right on a line between the top and bottom points.

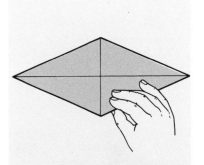

5 This should be the result.

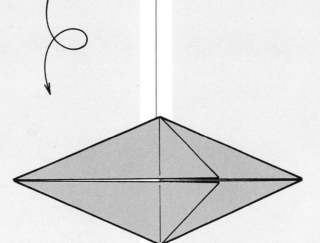

6 Turn the paper over, to make the fish base in its 'opened' form. (Note that the base's two triangular flaps are pointing towards the right.)

TATO (Traditional)

This traditional type of Japanese folded purse makes an ideal container for all sorts of small items, including needles, postage stamps and coins. Tato can also be folded from other regular shapes, such as pentagons and hexagons.

Use a square of paper, white side up.

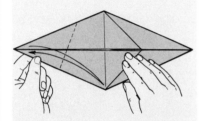

1 Begin with a fish base in its 'opened' form (see page 77). Valley fold the left-hand point down to meet the bottom point. Press it flat and unfold it.

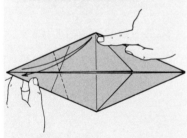

2 Valley fold the left-hand point up to meet the top point. Press it flat and unfold it.

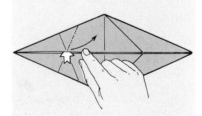

3 Open out the top left-hand layer of paper and . . .

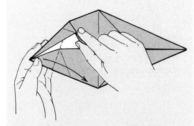

4 at the same time swing the left-hand point down to meet the bottom point.

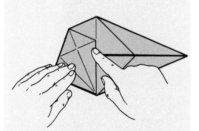

5 Press the paper flat into this position.

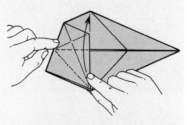

6 Valley fold the point up along the middle to meet the top point, at the same time . . .

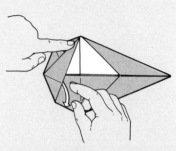

7 letting the paper arrange itself into a sort of petal fold. Press it flat. Pull the inside layer of paper . . .

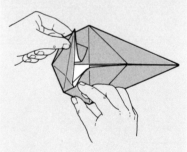

8 out and press it down neatly, thereby making . . .

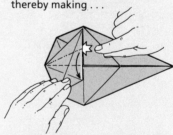

9 a triangular flap. Open out the flap and squash it down neatly into a diamond.

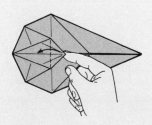

10 Valley fold the flap's tip over as shown, thereby making a white triangle.

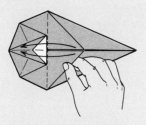

11 Valley fold the fish base's triangular flaps over to the left-hand side.

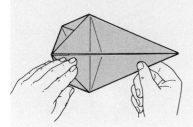

12 Repeat steps 1 to 10 with the right-hand point.

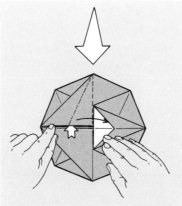

13 Open out the top fish base flap and squash it down neatly into a diamond.

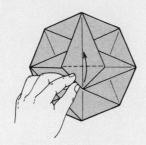

14 Repeat step 10.

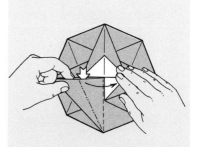

15 Repeat steps 13 and 14 with the bottom fish base flap.

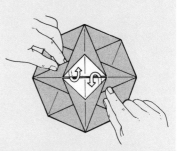

16 Arrange the white triangles to fit one over the other.

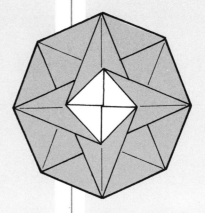

17 Here is the completed tato. To open the tato, pull opposite triangles apart.

DRAGON *(Kenji Jinbo)*

Kenji Jinbo was about 13½ years old when he created this dragon for his younger brother, thereby proving that you are never too old or too young to create your own origami. This model is made by combining a fish base, an off-centre fish base and a windmill base.

Use two squares of paper, identical in size, for the body and wings. For the head, use a square that is a quarter the size of the other squares. You will also need a tube of paper glue.

HEAD

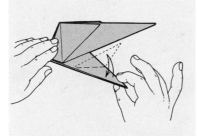

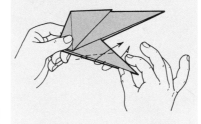

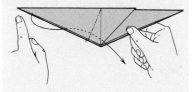

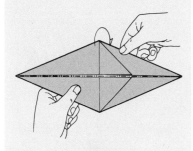

1 Begin with a fish base in its 'opened' form (see page 77). Mountain fold it in half from top to bottom.

2 Inside reverse fold the left-hand point into the position shown in step 3.

3 Valley fold the bottom right-hand point into the position shown by the dotted lines. Press it flat and unfold it.

4 Outside reverse fold the bottom right-hand point along the fold-lines made in step 3.

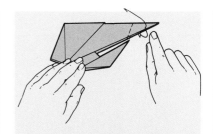

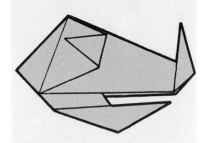

5 Outside reverse fold the top right-hand point.

6 Valley fold the triangular flap over towards the left, to suggest an eye. Repeat behind.

7 Here is the completed head.

BODY

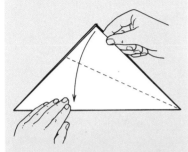

8 Turn a large square of paper around to look like a diamond, with the coloured side on top. Valley fold it in half from bottom to top, to make a triangle. From the bottom right-hand point, valley fold the top layer of paper down towards, but not to meet, the bottom edge.

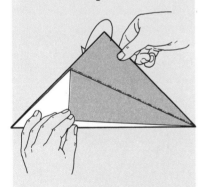

9 Repeat step 8 behind.

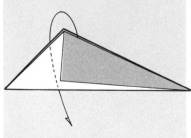

10 Unfold the paper . . .

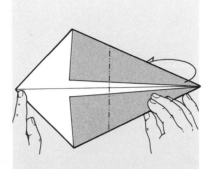

11 into this position. Mountain fold it in half from right to left.

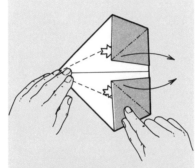

12 Pull the top and bottom flaps of paper over to the right, so their sloping edges come to rest slightly short of the middle fold-line. Press the paper flat, to make two triangular pointed flaps. This is an off-centre fish base.

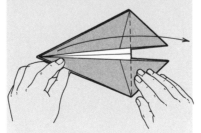

13 Valley fold the left-hand point over to the right on a line between the top and bottom points of the fish base.

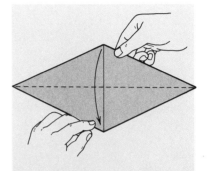

14 Valley fold the paper in half from top to bottom.

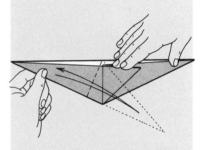

15 Valley fold the left-hand point into the position shown by the dotted lines. Press it flat and unfold it.

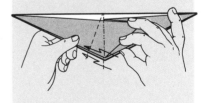

16 Step fold the left-hand point on either side by folding along the mountain and valley fold-lines as shown.

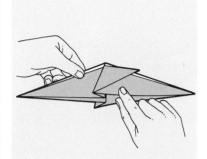

17 This should be the result.

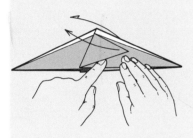

18 Flick the triangular flap over towards the left. Repeat behind.

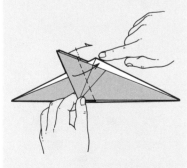

19 From the middle of the bottom edge, valley fold the triangular flap over to meet the top point. Repeat behind.

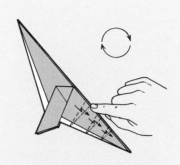

20 Turn the paper around. Make a series of valley and mountain folds along the right-hand point as shown. Press them . . .

21 flat and unfold them.

22 Along the fold-lines made in step 20, make a series of step folds on either side of the right-hand point.

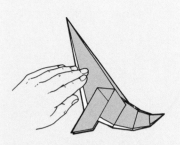

23 This should be the result.

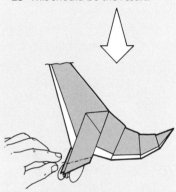

24 Mountain fold the bottom point upwards, to shape the back paw. Repeat behind.

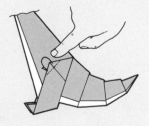

25 Shape the thigh with a small mountain fold. Repeat behind.

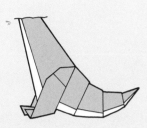

26 Here is the completed body.

WINGS AND FRONT PAWS

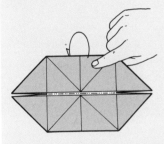

27 Begin with a windmill base (see page 42). Mountain fold it in half from top to bottom.

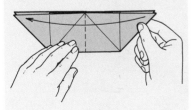

28 Valley fold the right-hand triangular point over to the other side, as though turning the page of a book, at the same time . . .

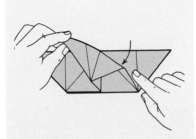

29 stretching and flattening down the middle layers of paper.

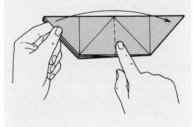

30 Return the triangular point to its original position.

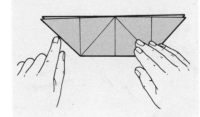

31 Repeat steps 28 to 30 with the left-hand triangular point.

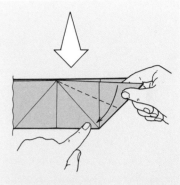

32 From the middle of the top edge, valley fold the right-hand triangular point down to lie along the adjacent diagonal fold-line.

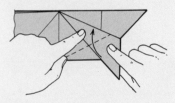

33 From the middle of the bottom edge, valley fold the bottom right-hand point up into the position shown in step 34.

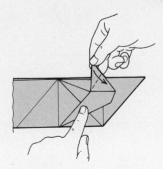

34 Valley fold the point's tip over and towards the right.

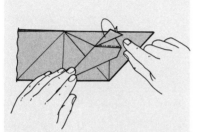

35 Mountain fold the point behind, to make a triangular pocket.

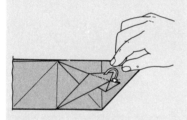

36 Insert the small protruding point into the pocket with a mountain fold, to complete a paw.

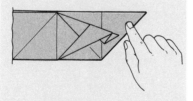

37 Repeat steps 32 to 36 behind.

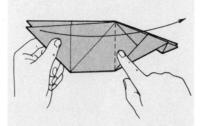

38 Valley fold the left-hand triangular point over to the right, as though turning the page of a book.

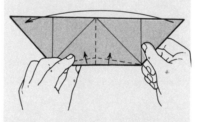

39 Lift the bottom edge up, to make a shallow tent-like valley fold, at the same time valley folding the right-hand triangular point over to the left.

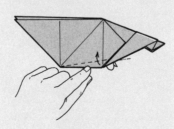

40 Valley fold the bottom point up on a slant. Repeat behind.

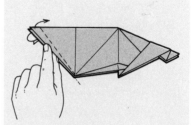

41 Valley fold a little of the left-hand sloping edge over, to give the wing a little character. Repeat behind.

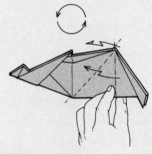

42 Turn the wings around. Step fold the top wing as shown. Repeat behind.

43 Open out the wings a little.

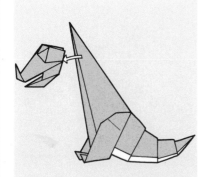

44 Glue the dragon's head on to its body.

45 Slit the top point as shown, to make the ears.

46 Open out the ears a little.

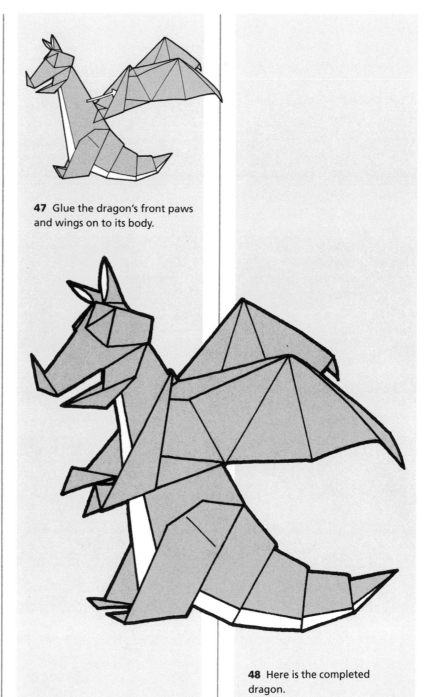

47 Glue the dragon's front paws and wings on to its body.

48 Here is the completed dragon.

MASK (Traditional)

By making slight variations in the folds you can easily create the recognizable mask of someone you know.

Use a square of paper, white side up.

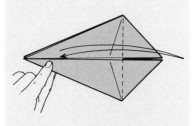

1 Begin with a fish base in its 'closed' form (see page 77). Valley fold the top left-hand point over to the right on a line between the top and bottom points. Press it flat and unfold it.

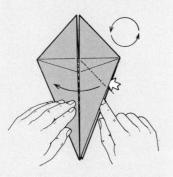

2 Turn the base around, so the flaps are pointing upwards. Insert your finger into the right-hand sloping edge and . . .

3 open it out, at the same time bringing the triangular flap down towards you.

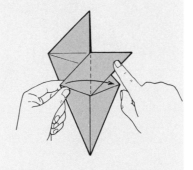

4 Press the flap down neatly. Valley fold the sloping edge back to its original position.

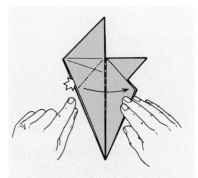

5 Insert your finger into the left-hand sloping edge and repeat steps 3 and 4.

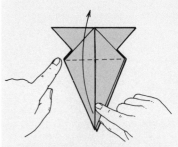

6 Valley fold the bottom point up on a line between the two side points.

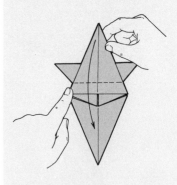

7 Valley fold the point down into the position shown in step 8, to make a pleat in the paper.

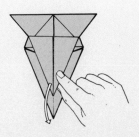

8 Unfold the point back to the position it was in at the beginning of step 6.

9 Changing the direction of the fold-lines made in steps 6 and 7, step fold the point up inside the model.

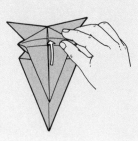

10 Step 9 is easier if the model is opened out. Press the paper flat, thereby slightly rearranging the top of the step fold.

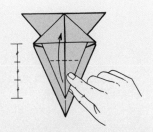

11 Valley fold the point up as far as shown, to make the nose and upper jaw.

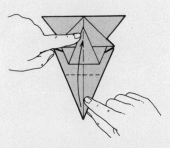

12 Valley fold the remaining bottom point up to meet the tip of the previous one.

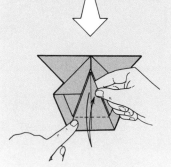

13 Valley fold what was originally the bottom point down and along the bottom of the jaw. Press it flat and unfold it.

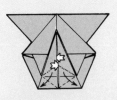

14 Open out the point, at the same time . . .

15 valley folding its tip down towards you, to make the lower jaw and suggest a beard.

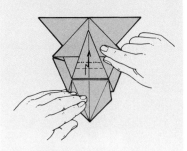

16 Step fold the nose and . . .

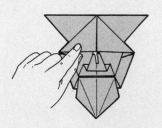

17 tuck its tip underneath the horizontal edge.

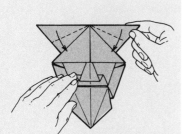

18 Valley fold the triangular flaps down to lie along the sides of the head.

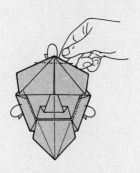

19 Shape the top of the head and the sides of the face with mountain folds.

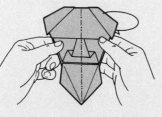

20 Mountain fold the model in half from right to left.

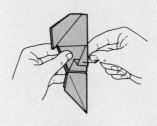

21 Pinch the nose and . . .

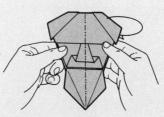

22 pull it away from the face. Open out the model, but do not press it flat.

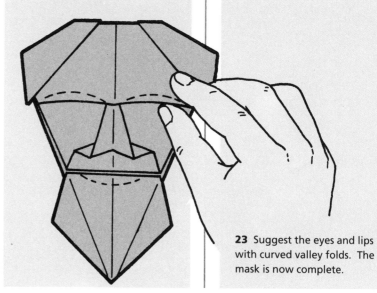

23 Suggest the eyes and lips with curved valley folds. The mask is now complete.

PROPELLER PLANE
(Seiji Nishikawa)

This piece of origami is made by combining half a pig base and a fish base. As with all origami models, try changing the angle of the folds, especially those of the tail, wings and propeller, to see how many new shapes you can create.

Use two squares of paper, identical in size.

MAIN WINGS

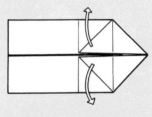

1 Begin with the square's coloured side on top and fold half a pig base (see page 29) on its right-hand side. Pinch the triangular points and stretch them apart, thereby taking the right-hand side point into the middle and at the same time flattening it out.

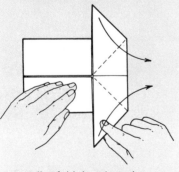

2 Valley fold the triangular points over to the right.

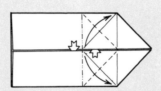

3 On the top layer of paper, make the valley and mountain folds as shown, thereby opening it out.

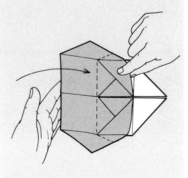

4 Take the opened layer over to the right and . . .

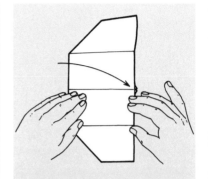

5 flatten it down into the shape of a house.

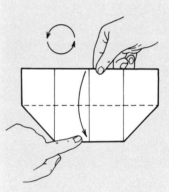

6 Turn the paper around into this position. Valley fold the top layer of paper in half from top to bottom.

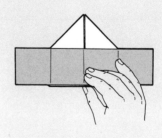

7 This should be the result.

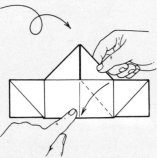

8 Turn the paper over. Valley fold the right-hand triangular point down, so its vertical edge lies along the bottom edge.

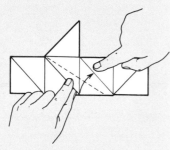

9 Valley fold the bottom point up on a slant.

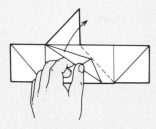

10 Return the triangular point to its original position, but do not unfold the previous step.

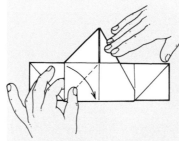

11 Repeat steps 8 to 10 with the left-hand triangular point. Later on these points will become the propellers.

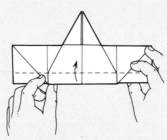

12 Valley fold the bottom layers of paper up and along a line that uses the top of the short vertical edges as its location point.

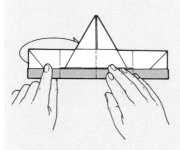

13 Mountain fold the paper in half from left to right, thereby . . .

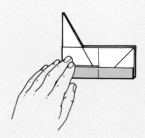

14 completing the main wings.

AIRFRAME

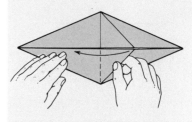

15 Begin with a fish base in its 'opened' form (see page 77). Valley fold the bottom triangular flap over towards the left on a line between the top and bottom points.

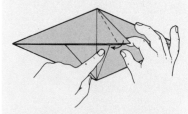

16 Valley fold the top triangular flap over to the point where the bottom sloping fold-line meets the horizontal middle line.

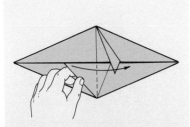

17 Return the bottom triangular flap to its original position.

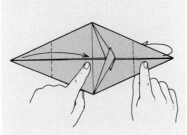

18 Repeat step 16 with the bottom triangular flap. Valley fold the left-hand side point and mountain fold the right-hand side point into the middle.

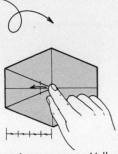

19 Turn the paper over. Valley fold the middle point over as far as shown.

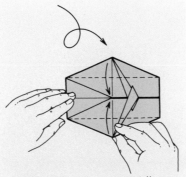

20 Turn the paper over. Valley fold the top and bottom points into the middle.

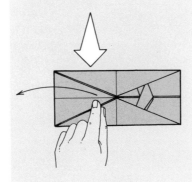

21 Return the left-hand side point to its original position.

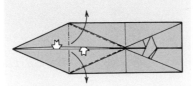

22 Reach inside and open out the layers of the left-hand side point, at the same time . . .

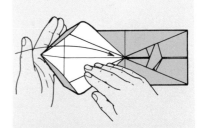

23 valley folding its tip into the middle.

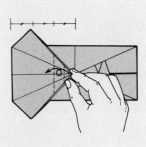

24 Valley fold the tip over and over as far as shown, to make what will later become the back wheel.

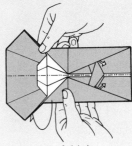

25 Mountain fold the paper in half from bottom to top, at the same time releasing the right-hand flaps. Later on, these flaps will become the front wheels.

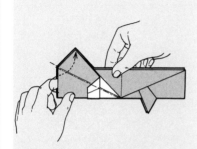

26 Inside reverse fold the bottom left-hand corner up on a line between the middle and the top of the left-hand side.

27 Fold the left-hand flap down, so the tail appears. Repeat behind.

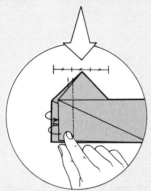

28 Mountain fold the left-hand side into the tail section as far as shown. Repeat behind.

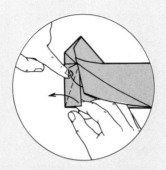

29 Looking inside the tail section, valley fold the bottom layer of paper out on a slant. Repeat with the top layer, to make the tail flaps.

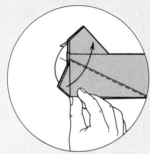

30 Valley fold the top tail flap up and along the existing sloping fold-line. Repeat behind.

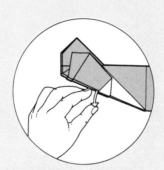

31 Pull the back wheel down from inside (see step 24) and press it flat . . .

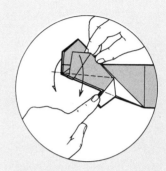

32 into this position. Valley fold the top tail flap down on a line between the top of the wheel and the bottom of the left-hand side. Repeat behind.

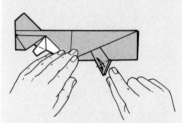

33 Valley fold the wheel's tip up as shown. Press it flat and unfold it. This is in preparation for a squash fold.

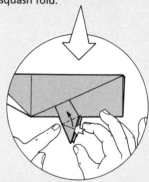

34 Using the fold-line that has just been made, open out and squash the wheel down neatly into a diamond.

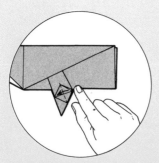

35 Valley fold the wheel in half from side to side, thereby making

36 a white diamond. Repeat steps 33 to 36 behind.

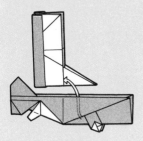

37 Insert the point that is inside the airframe (see step 19) as far as it will go into the main wing. Make sure the point goes between the propellers and the wings.

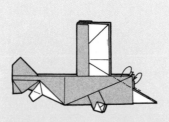

38 Shape the cockpit with a mountain fold. Repeat behind.

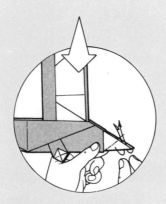

39 Mountain fold the top propeller so it points upwards. Repeat behind.

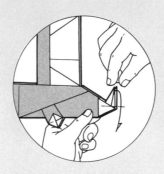

40 Mountain fold the top propeller so it points downwards.

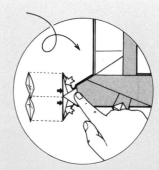

41 Turn the model over. Open out and indent the propellers slightly, to make them three-dimensional.

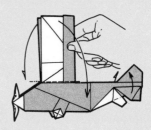

42 On either side of the model valley fold the main wings down and valley fold the tail flaps up, so they are horizontal to the airframe.

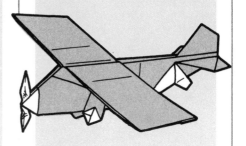

43 Here is the completed propeller plane.

BLINTZ BASE
(Traditional)

When the four corners of a square of paper have been folded into the middle, we say that the paper has been 'blintzed'. This is a Yiddish word which has its origins in the Ukraine, and a blintz is a thin pancake which contains cottage cheese or some other filling, with its corners folded into the middle. The word 'blintz' was introduced into origami vocabulary by New York paperfolders during the 1950s. In Japan the technique of folding the four corners into the middle is used in cushion making, so this base is also called the cushion fold. To make a blintz base, use a square of paper, white side up, and follow the instructions opposite.

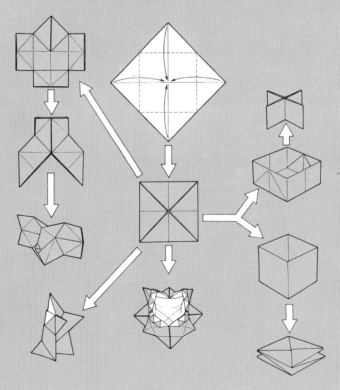

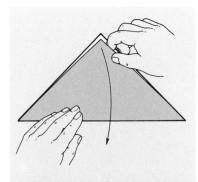

1 Begin with a diaper fold (see page 50). Unfold it completely.

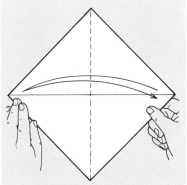

2 Valley fold the paper in half from side to side. Press it flat and unfold it.

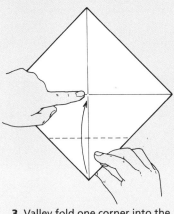

3 Valley fold one corner into the middle.

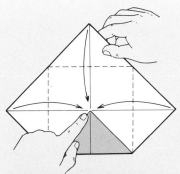

4 Valley fold the remaining corners into the middle. Press the paper flat.

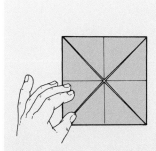

5 Here is the completed blintz base.

BOX *(Traditional)*

Origami boxes come in all shapes and sizes. This one is ideal as a desk tidy, because it can hold any small items of stationery that may be lying around.

Use a square of paper, white side up.

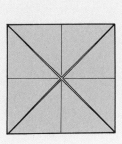

1 Begin with a blintz base (see above).

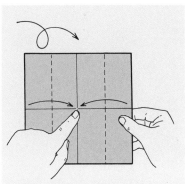

2 Turn the base over. Valley fold the sides over to meet the middle fold-line.

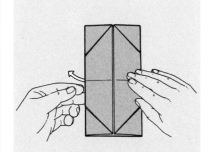

3 Release the left-hand corner from underneath and . . .

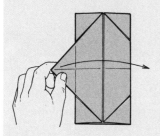

4 take it over to the opposite side.

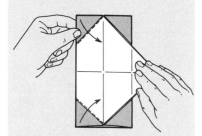

5 Valley fold the top and bottom corners over to meet the adjacent fold-line.

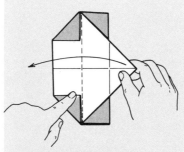

6 Return the corner to its original position and, . . .

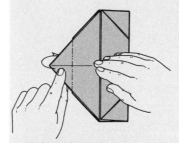

7 along the existing vertical fold-line, mountain fold it behind.

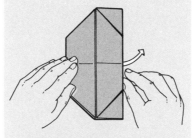

8 Release the right-hand corner from underneath and repeat steps 4 to 7.

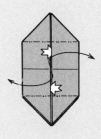

9 This should be the result. Put your fingers underneath the layers of paper.

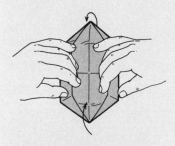

10 Carefully pull your hands apart. The paper will open out into a box. You can make it firm and strong by pinching together the corners and sides of the box.

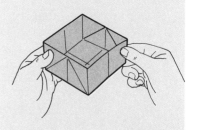

11 Here is the completed box.

PARTITION FOR A BOX
(*Traditional*)

This fold is a very good example of how logical thinking helps to create a piece of origami.

Use two squares of paper, identical in size, white sides up.

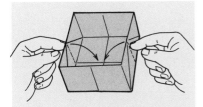

1 Begin by folding both squares into boxes (see opposite). Press down on the opposite sides of one box (you might have to . . .

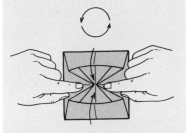

2 turn it around a little so this move can take place) and collapse them into the middle as shown. Press the paper flat.

3 Mountain fold the paper in half from top to bottom.

4 Valley fold the right-hand side over to the other side, as though turning the page of a book, at the same time . . .

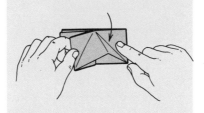

5 stretching and flattening down the middle layers of paper.

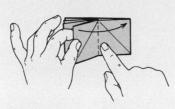

6 Return the side to its original position.

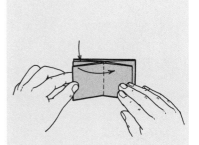

7 Repeat steps 4 to 6 with the left-hand side.

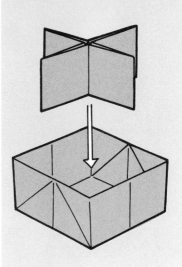

8 Arrange the model into a cross-like shape, to complete the partition. Insert it into the remaining box as shown.

BOX AND PURSE *(Traditional)*

These models are very easy to make. Do not be discouraged by the tricky folds in steps 9 to 13; they all fall into place very easily. Use a square of paper, white side up.

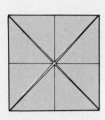

1 Begin with a blintz base (see page 95).

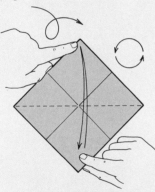

2 Turn the base over and around. Valley fold it in half from bottom to top. Press it flat and unfold it.

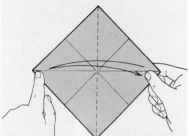

3 Valley fold the paper in half from side to side. Press it flat and unfold it.

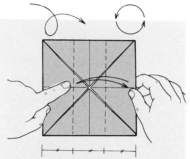

4 Turn the paper over and around. Valley fold the right-hand side over to a point one-third of the way to the other side. Press it flat and unfold it.

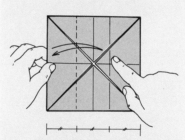

5 Valley fold the left-hand side over to meet the fold-line made in step 4. Press flat and unfold it.

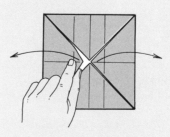

6 Unfold the two middle corners as shown.

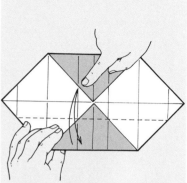

7 Valley fold the bottom edge up to a point one-third of the distance to the top edge. Press it flat and unfold it.

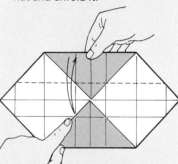

8 Valley fold the top edge down to meet the fold-line made in step 7. Press it flat and unfold it.

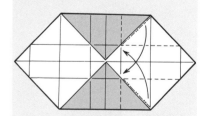

9 Using the existing valley and mountain fold-lines . . .

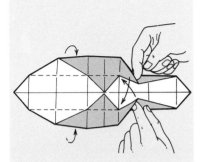

10 form the right-hand side of the box.

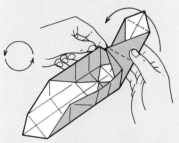

11 Once again using the existing valley and mountain fold-lines, fold the side . . .

12 into the box, thereby locking all the folds together. Repeat steps 9 and 10 at the opposite end of the paper, to form the box's left-hand side.

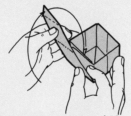

13 Repeat steps 11 and 12.

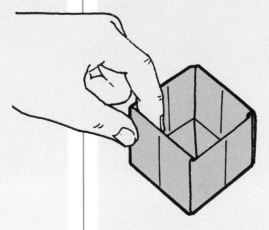

14 Here is the completed box.

PURSE

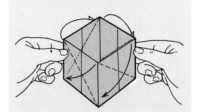

15 Push the sides of the box in the direction shown by the arrows, keeping the base still (this move is very easy to do).

16 The paper will suddenly collapse into this position. Press it flat, to complete the purse. To open, twist opposite edges apart.

FANCY BOX *(Traditional)*

It is thought that this model was originally made in Japan, but that the pleated decorations were added later by a Spanish paperfolder. The fancy box makes an ideal container for sweets, pretzels or other party favourites.

Use a square of paper, white side up.

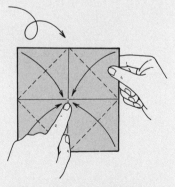

1 Begin with a blintz base (see page 95).

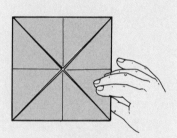

2 Turn the base over. Valley fold the corners into the middle.

3 Valley fold the corners out, so they . . .

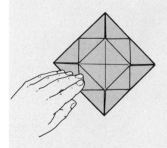

4 are aligned with the edges.

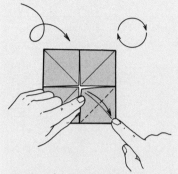

5 Turn the paper over and around, so it looks like a square. Valley fold the front flap of one small square in half from the middle to the corner, to make a triangle.

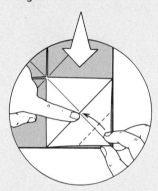

6 Start pleating. Valley fold the flap's tip over to meet the base of the triangle.

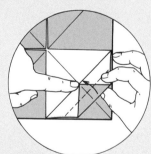

7 Repeat step 6 with the newly made edge.

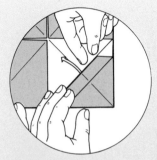

8 Pull out the inside triangle.

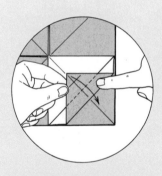

9 Valley fold the triangle over and along the fold-line made in step 7.

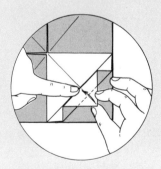

10 Valley fold the tip towards the middle and along the fold-line made in step 7.

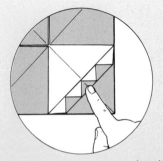

11 This corner is now completed.

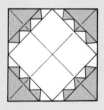

12 Repeat steps 5 to 10 with the remaining three small squares.

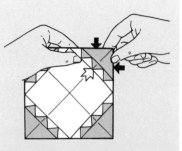

13 Open out a corner by pressing its sides together, at the same time . . .

14 inserting your forefinger inside as shown. Repeat steps 13 and 14 with the remaining three corners.

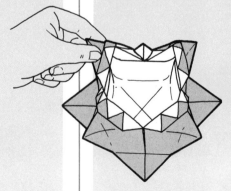

15 Firm up the folds around the sides and base to complete the fancy box.

YAKKO-SAN *(Traditional)*

Yakko-san is believed to be one of the oldest models known in origami. It is supposed to represent a person dressed in a kimono.

Use a square of paper, white side up.

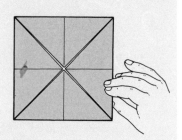

1 Begin with a blintz base (see page 95).

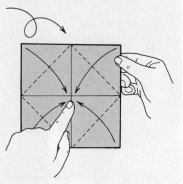

2 Turn the base over. Valley fold the corners into . . .

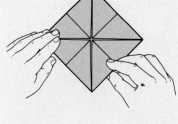

3 the middle.

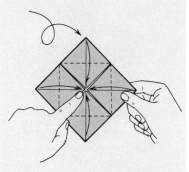

4 Turn the paper over. Once again, valley fold the corners into . . .

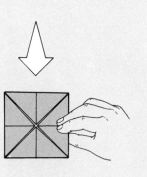

5 the middle.

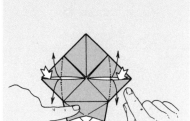

6 Turn the paper over and around, so it looks like a diamond. Open out the bottom square and . . .

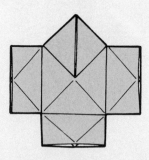

7 press it down neatly into a rectangle. Repeat with the right- and left-hand squares.

8 Here is the completed Yakko-san. Can you see his coat, sleeves and diamond-shaped face?

HAKAMA AND CAMERA
(Traditional)

Using Yakko-san as your foundation, you can develop two further models that are connected to each other. Why not experiment and create your own Yakko-san-based models?

Use a square of paper, white side up.

HAKAMA (Pleated trousers)

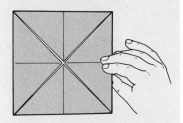

1 Begin with a blintz base (see page 95).

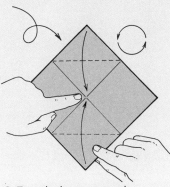

2 Turn the base over and around, so it looks like a diamond. Valley fold the top and bottom corners into the middle.

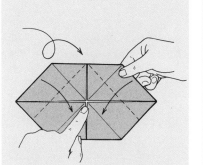

3 Turn the paper over. Valley fold the right- and left-hand halves of the top edge down to meet the middle fold-line.

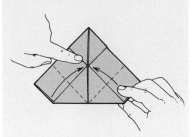

4 Valley fold the right- and left-hand halves of the bottom edge up to meet the middle fold-line.

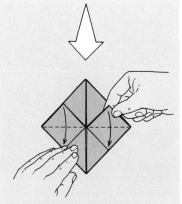

5 Valley fold the side points down as shown, to make two triangular flaps.

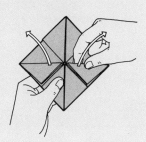

6 Pinch the flaps and pull their outer layers apart, to make . . .

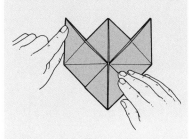

7 two triangular points.

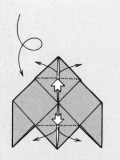

8 Turn the paper over. Open out the top and bottom squares and press them down neatly into rectangles.

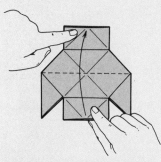

9 Valley fold the paper in half from bottom to top. Press it flat.

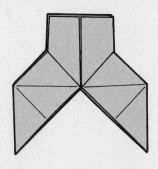

10 Here is the completed Hakama.

CAMERA

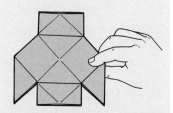

11 Begin with a completed step 8 of the Hakama.

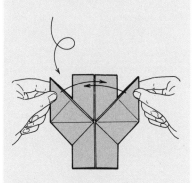

12 Turn the paper over. Place the triangular points on top of each other, so their tips slightly cross over.

13 Fold the tips over as shown, to lock the triangular points together.

14 Here is the completed camera.

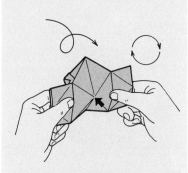

15 To 'take a picture', turn the camera over and around. Hold it as shown and press where indicated with your thumb, to make the two locked tips come apart with a . . .

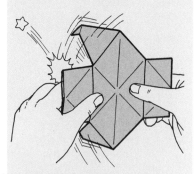

16 'click'! If you do not get a click first time around, then check that the tips were not taken too far across in step 12.

SUMO WRESTLING GAME
(Traditional)

An interesting origami technique is to make models that have some sort of movement to them. Many such models are pressed, pulled or blown to make them move. This model is unique, because it relies upon vibrations for its source of movement.

Use a square of paper, white side up.

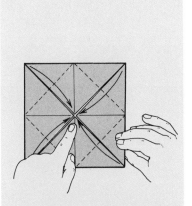

1 Begin with a blintz base (see page 95). Valley fold the corners into . . .

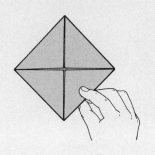

2 the middle.

3 Turn the paper over. Valley fold over the top point's sloping edges so they lie along the middle fold-line, while at the same time . . .

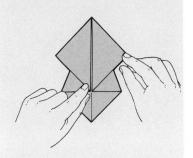

4 letting the corners flick up from underneath.

5 Valley fold the top point down on a line between the two side points.

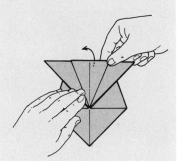

6 Release the corner from underneath.

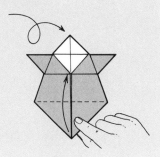

7 Turn the paper over. Valley fold the bottom point up on a line between the two side points, to make a triangle.

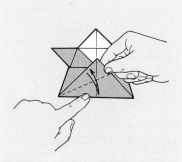

8 Valley fold the triangle's left-hand sloping edge down to meet the bottom edge. Press it flat and unfold it.

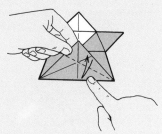

9 Repeat step 8 with the right-hand sloping edge.

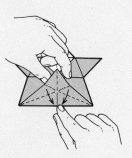

10 Pinch together the sloping edges along the fold-lines made in steps 8 and 9, to fold the triangle into a rabbit ear.

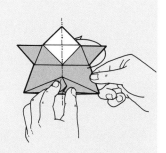

11 Mountain fold the paper in half from right to left.

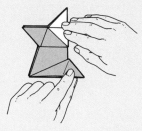

12 Here is the completed Sumo wrestler. Now make another one.

HOW TO PLAY

13 Draw a circle on the top of an empty box to make the wrestling ring.

14 Position the wrestlers inside the ring, face to face. Tap the box with your fingertips. The wrestler who falls over or is pushed out of the ring loses the game.

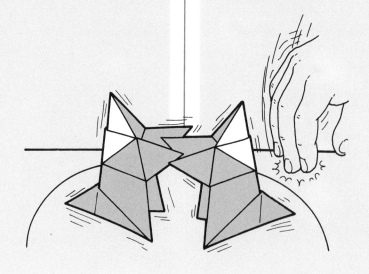

WATERBOMB BASE
(Traditional)

The waterbomb base is so called because it is the starting point for the traditional waterbomb (see page 109). In Japan this base is known as the balloon base. There are several ways to fold a waterbomb base. To make the one overleaf, use a square of paper, white side up.

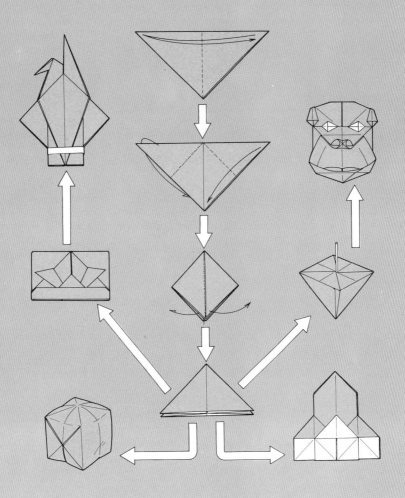

WATERBOMB BASE

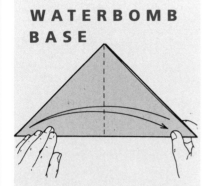

1 Begin with a diaper fold (see page 50). Valley fold it in half from side to side. Press it flat and unfold it.

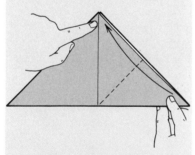

2 Valley fold the bottom right-hand point up . . .

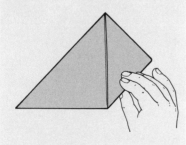

3 to meet the top point.

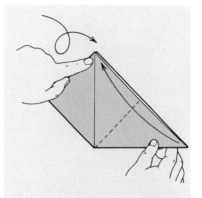

4 Turn the paper over. Repeat step 2.

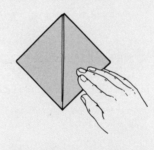

5 Press the paper flat.

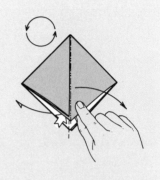

6 Turn the paper around. Separate the front layer from the back layer, to let . . .

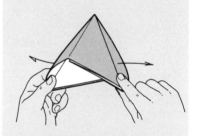

7 the two side points come together.

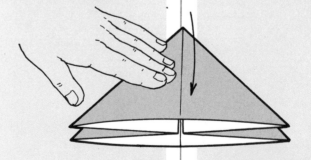

8 Press the paper down neatly into a triangle. This completes the waterbomb base.

WATERBOMB (Traditional)

The waterbomb, like the Yakko-san, is thought to be one of the oldest models known in origami. It has been suggested that this model may have originated in ancient China. In Japan the waterbomb is also called the balloon, because there they are thrown at parties or hung up as decorations during a festival. When made from colourful paper the waterbomb is an ideal Christmas tree decoration.

Use a square of paper, white side up.

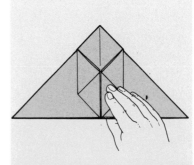

5 This should be the result. Turn the paper over. Repeat steps 1 to 4.

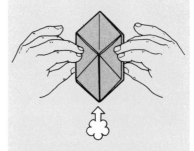

6 Hold the paper loosely and blow gently into the small hole that you will find at the bottom point. The paper will open out and look like a balloon.

1 Begin with a waterbomb base (see opposite). Valley fold the bottom points up to meet the top point.

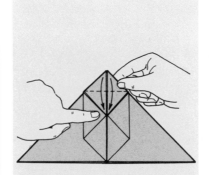

3 Valley fold the top points into the middle, to make two triangular flaps.

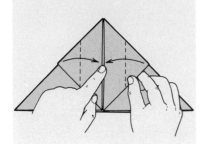

2 Valley fold the right- and left-hand side points into the middle.

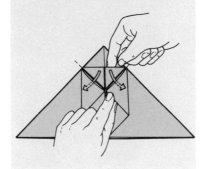

4 Tuck these flaps into the adjacent pockets with a valley fold.

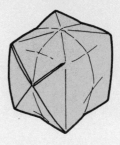

7 Here is the completed waterbomb.

CHURCH *(Traditional)*

When made in miniature this charming fold looks perfect and is ideal for gluing on to your personal stationery.

Use a square of paper, white side up.

1 Begin with a waterbomb base (see page 108). Valley fold the bottom points up to meet the top point.

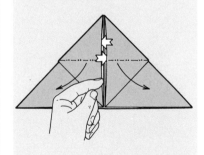

2 Open out and squash the right-hand point . . .

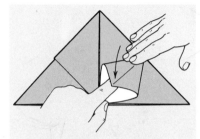

3 down neatly into a square.

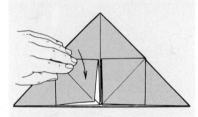

4 Repeat steps 2 and 3 with the left-hand point.

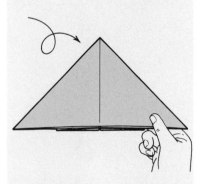

5 Turn the paper over. Repeat steps 1 to 4.

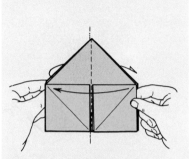

6 Valley fold the right-hand layer of paper over to the left, as though turning the page of a book. Repeat behind.

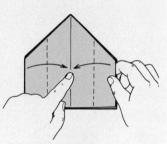

7 Valley fold the right- and left-hand sides over to meet the middle fold-line.

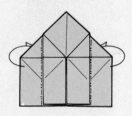

8 Repeat step 7 behind.

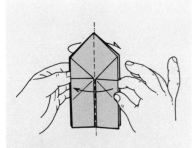

9 Repeat step 6.

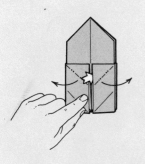

10 Open out and squash the right-hand layer of paper . . .

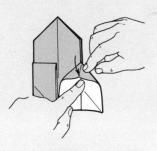

11 down neatly into the shape of a triangular roof.

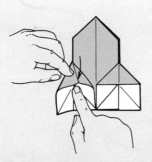

12 Repeat steps 10 to 11 with the left-hand layer of paper.

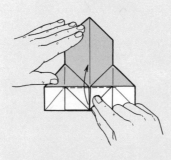

13 Valley fold the middle point up . . .

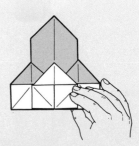

14 towards the top point.

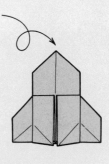

15 Turn the paper over. Repeat steps 10 to 14.

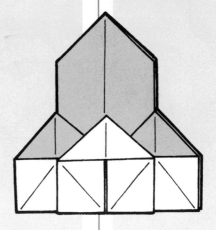

16 Here is the completed church.

SPINNING TOP *(Steve Biddle)*

Steps 5 and 6 of this model are slightly tricky so do take your time when folding it.

Use a square of paper, white side up.

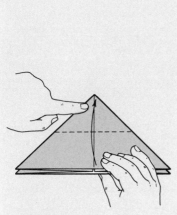

1 Begin with a waterbomb base (see page 108). Valley fold it in half from bottom to top.

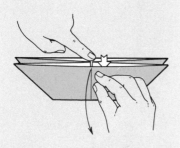

2 Fold the top layer of paper down, to make . . .

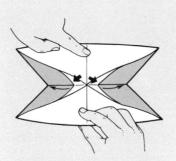

3 the inside layers rise up. Flatten the folded edge of each layer . . .

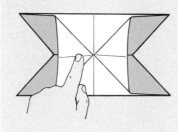

4 to form squash folds.

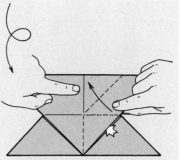

5 Turn the paper over. Twist the top right-hand layer of paper anti-clockwise through a quarter of a turn, so the mountain fold-line meets the middle of the top edge.

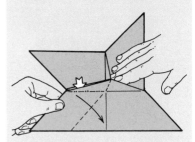

6 Repeat step 5 with the lower left-hand layer of paper, so the mountain fold-line meets the middle of the bottom edge.

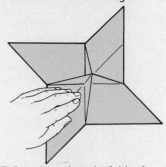

7 Press into place the folds of the central star (shaped like a waterbomb base), so it is positioned centrally on the adjoining platform of paper.

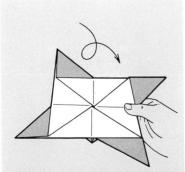

8 Turn the paper over.

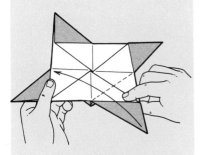

9 Valley fold the bottom right-hand triangular point over to meet the middle of the left-hand side.

10 Valley fold the bottom left-hand triangular point up to meet the middle of the top edge.

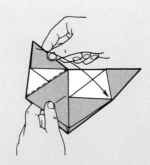

11 Valley fold the top left-hand triangular point over to meet the middle of the right-hand side.

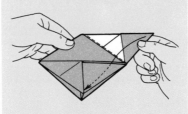

12 Finally, valley fold the top right-hand triangular point down to meet what was originally the middle of the bottom edge, at the same time tucking it underneath the adjacent layer of paper as shown. This locks all the points together.

13 Insert a cocktail stick into the middle of the model.

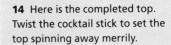

14 Here is the completed top. Twist the cocktail stick to set the top spinning away merrily.

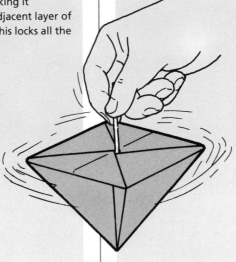

KABUTO WRAPPER *(Traditional)*

In Japan this model is called a 'noshi' (wrapper). A noshi is a folded paper object which Japanese sales people fasten to a purchase when they know it will be given as a gift. The noshi signifies the wishes of the giver that the recipient will have good fortune — a custom whose origins date back to the end of the twelfth century.

Use a rectangle of paper, about A4 in size, white side up.

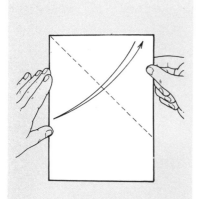

1 Place the rectangle lengthways on. Valley fold the top edge over to lie along the left-hand side. Press it flat and unfold it.

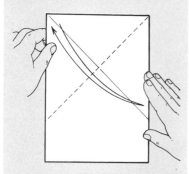

2 Valley fold the top edge over to lie along the right-hand side. Press it flat and unfold it.

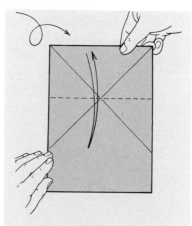

3 Turn the paper over. Valley fold the top edge down to meet the bottom of the diagonal fold-lines. Press it flat and unfold it.

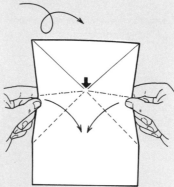

4 Turn the paper over. Press the middle of the fold-lines, until the sides pop up. Bring the sides together and . . .

5 down towards you. Press the top down neatly . . .

6 into a triangle, thereby making a waterbomb base in one end of the paper.

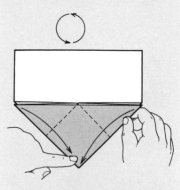

7 Turn the paper around. Valley fold the side points down to meet the bottom point.

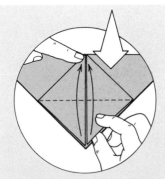

8 Repeat steps 3 and 4 of the kabuto (see page 56).

9 Repeat steps 5 to 7 of the kabuto (see page 56).

10 This should be the result.

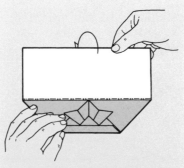

11 Mountain fold the top rectangle of paper behind and along the base of the waterbomb.

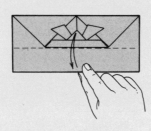

12 Valley fold the bottom rectangle of paper up and along the kabuto's base. Press it flat and unfold it. Then along the same fold-line . . .

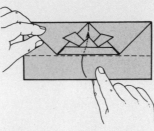

13 tuck it underneath the kabuto.

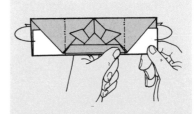

14 Mountain fold the sides behind, taking in just a little of the kabuto's base material.

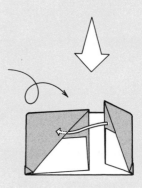

15 Turn the paper over. Insert one side into the other. Press the paper flat.

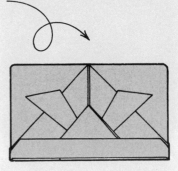

16 Turn the model over, thereby completing the kabuto wrapper.

CRANE WRAPPER *(Traditional)*

The crane is probably the most well-known of all origami models. It is often used throughout the world as a symbol of peace.

Use a rectangle of paper, about A4 in size, white side up.

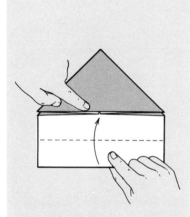

1 Begin with a completed step 6 of the kabuto wrapper (see page 114). Valley fold the bottom rectangle of paper in half.

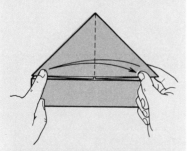

2 Valley fold the waterbomb base in half from side to side. Press it flat and unfold it.

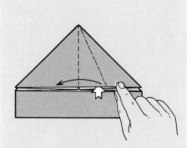

3 Open out the right-hand point and . . .

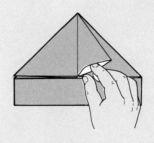

4 squash it down neatly . . .

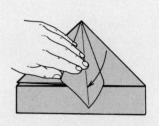

5 into a diamond.

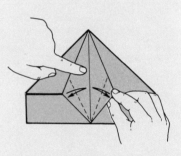

6 Valley fold the squashed point's lower sloping edges over, so they lie along the middle fold-line. Press them flat and unfold them, thereby preparing the paper for a petal fold.

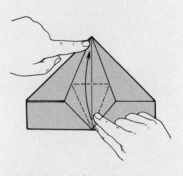

7 Pinch and lift up the bottom point's tip.

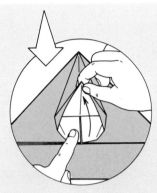

8 Continue to lift up the point, so . . .

9 its edges meet in the middle. Press the paper flat, to make it diamond-shaped. This completes the petal fold.

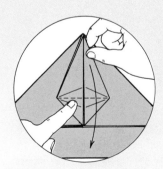

10 Valley fold the petal fold down as far as it will go.

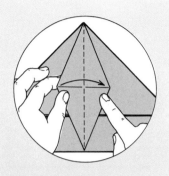

11 Valley fold the petal fold in half from side to side.

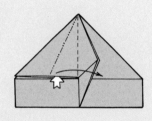

12 Repeat steps 3 to 11 with the left-hand point.

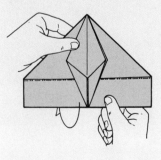

13 Mountain fold the bottom rectangle of paper behind and . . .

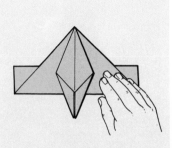

14 along the base of the waterbomb.

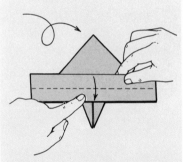

15 Turn the paper over. Valley fold the rectangle of paper in half from top to bottom.

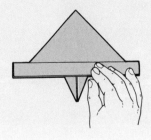

16 Press the paper flat.

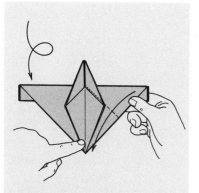

17 Turn the paper over. Valley fold the right-hand half of the top edge down to meet the middle fold-line, at the same time . . .

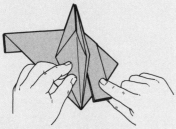

18 taking it underneath the petal fold.

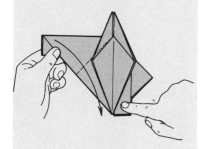

19 Repeat steps 17 and 18 with the left-hand half of the top edge.

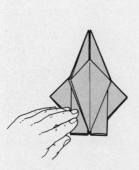

20 This should be the result.

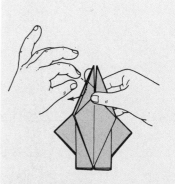

21 Inside reverse fold the tip of the left-hand point, to make the crane's head.

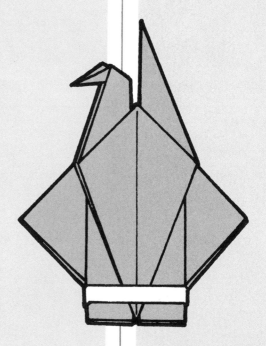

22 Slide a band of gold paper around the bottom layers of paper, thereby completing the crane wrapper.

GORILLA *(Atsushi Miyashita)*

When making this model, try hard to find the right colour and texture of paper, as this will enhance the finished item and make it look more realistic.

Use a square of paper, white side up.

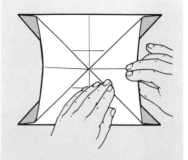

5 to form squash folds.

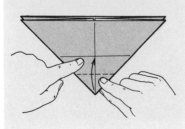

1 Begin with a waterbomb base (see page 108). Turn it around and valley fold it in half from bottom to top. Press it flat and unfold it.

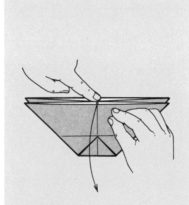

3 Fold the top layer of paper down, so that . . .

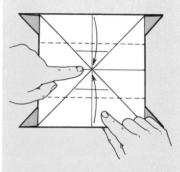

6 Valley fold the top and bottom edges over to meet the middle fold-line.

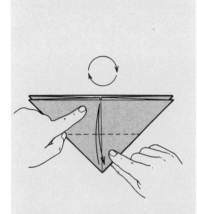

2 Valley fold the bottom point up to meet the fold-line made in step 1.

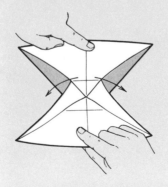

4 the inside layers rise up. Flatten the folded edge of each layer . . .

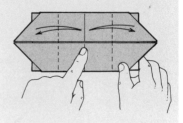

7 Valley fold the partially visible sides (not the points) over to meet the middle fold-line. Press them flat and unfold them.

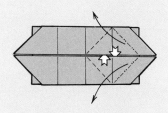

8 On the right-hand layer of paper, make the valley and mountain folds as shown, thereby opening it out.

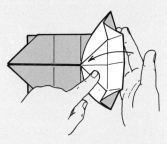

9 Take the opened layer into the middle and . . .

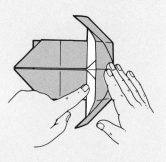

10 flatten it down into . . .

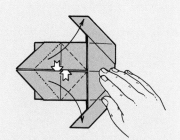

11 the shape of a roof. Repeat steps 8 to 11 with the left-hand layer of paper.

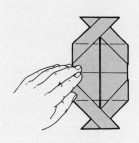

12 This should be the result.

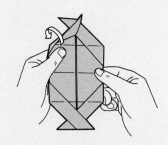

13 Turn the top left-hand band of paper inside out, thereby taking it behind.

14 Repeat step 13 with the remaining bands of paper.

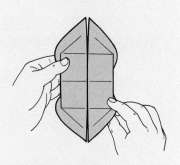

15 This should be the result.

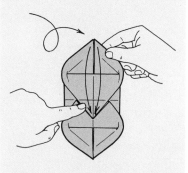

16 Turn the paper over. Valley fold the top points down and along the top horizontal edge.

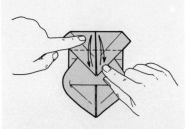

17 Valley fold the points in half from bottom to top. Press them flat and unfold them.

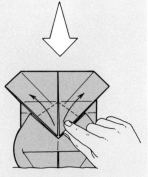

18 Valley fold the points out as shown.

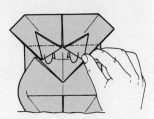

19 Along the fold-lines made in step 17, mountain fold the points behind, to make two small triangular flaps.

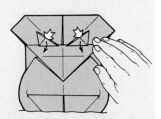

20 Open out and squash the triangular flaps down neatly.

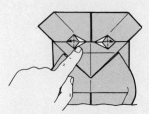

21 Valley fold the top flap of each squash fold out, to make the gorilla's eyes.

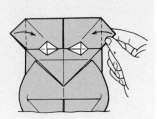

22 Valley fold the right- and left-hand side points over as shown.

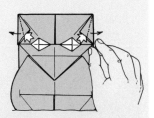

23 Open out and squash the side points down neatly, to make the gorilla's ears.

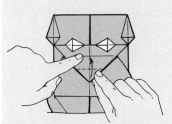

24 Valley fold the middle point in half.

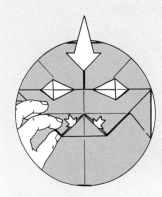

25 Place a finger into each side of the middle point as shown by the arrows . . .

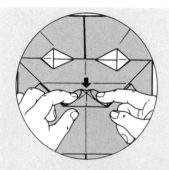

26 and pull forwards and down. As you pull, the middle point will slightly flatten itself, thereby . . .

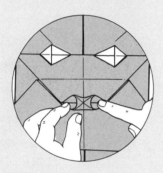

27 making the nose.

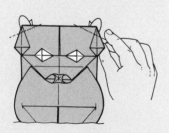

28 Shape either side of the head with a mountain fold.

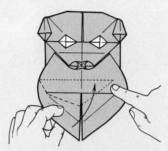

29 Valley fold the bottom left-hand point into the position shown by the dotted lines.

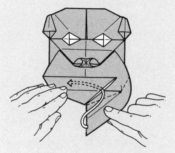

30 Repeat step 29 with the bottom right-hand point, but as you do so insert it inside the left-hand point, to make the gorilla's lower jaw.

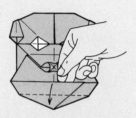

31 Valley fold the lower jaw down and along the existing horizontal fold-line, . . .

32 at the same time forming the cheeks. Valley fold the bottom horizontal edge of paper up slightly, to make the upper jaw.

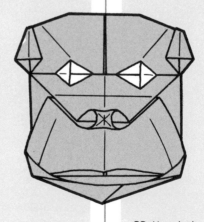

33 Here is the completed gorilla.

PRELIMINARY FOLD
(Traditional)

The preliminary fold is so called because it is the foundation for several bases, and therefore an infinite number of models. If it is turned inside out, it becomes the waterbomb base. By squashing and petal folding its four flaps, the frog base (see page 145) is created. If its front and back layers are petal folded, you make the bird base (see page 154). Because of its shape, the preliminary fold is known as the square base in Japan. There are several ways of making a preliminary fold. To make the version overleaf, use a square of paper, white side up.

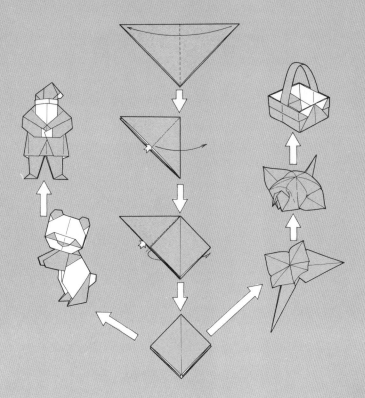

PRELIMINARY FOLD

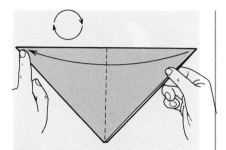

1 Begin with a diaper fold (see page 50). Turn it around, so it points towards you. Valley fold it in half from right to left.

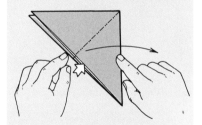

2 Lift the top half up along the middle fold-line. Open out the paper and . . .

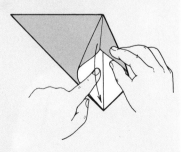

3 squash it down neatly . . .

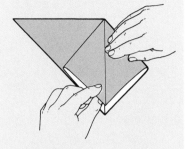

4 into a diamond.

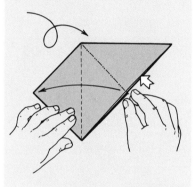

5 Turn the paper over. Repeat step 2.

6 Repeat steps 3 . . .

7 and 4, thereby completing the . . .

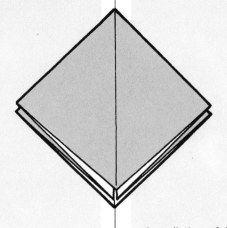

8 preliminary fold.

FAT SPARROW *(Traditional)*

This traditional model is very popular among Japanese children, but it is comparatively unknown here in the West. Compare it with the crane on page 157.

Use a square of paper, white side up.

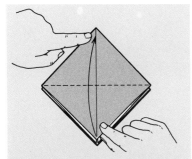

1 Begin with a preliminary fold (see opposite). Valley fold the front flap of paper in half from bottom to top.

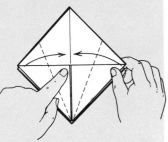

2 Valley fold the lower sloping edges over, so . . .

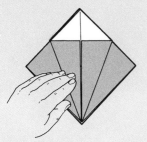

3 they lie along the vertical middle line.

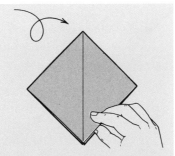

4 Turn the paper over. Repeat steps 1 and 2.

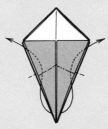

5 Make the sparrow's head and tail by inside reverse folding the bottom points. This is what you do. . . .

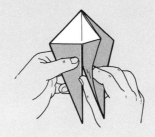

6 Pinch a bottom point and . . .

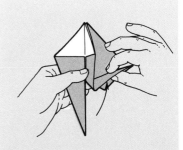

7 pull it up inside the model.

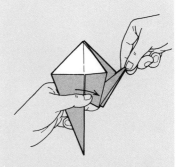

8 Press the paper flat into this position. Repeat steps 6 to 8 with the remaining bottom point.

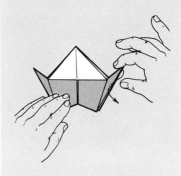

9 Inside reverse fold the tip of one of the top points, to make the beak.

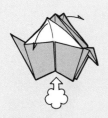

10 Pick up the model and inflate it by blowing gently into the small hole that you will find at the bottom, at the same time pulling the wings apart and flattening out the middle point a little.

11 Here is the completed fat sparrow.

FATHER CHRISTMAS
(Steve and Megumi Biddle)

We have adapted this model from one that was originally created by Steve Casey, an Australian paperfolder. For a creative challenge, see which other human figures you can invent, using step 26 as your starting point.

Use a square of paper, white side up.

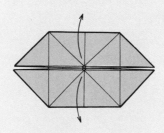

1 Begin with a windmill base (see page 42). Unfold it completely.

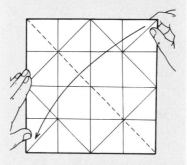

2 Valley fold the square in half from top right to bottom left, with the white side on top, thereby making a diaper fold.

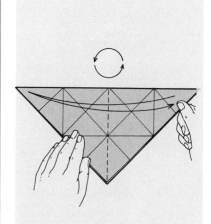

3 Turn the diaper fold around, so the tip is pointing towards you. Now make a preliminary fold (see page 124).

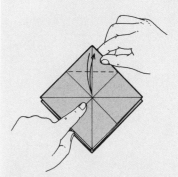

4 Valley fold the top point into the middle. Press it flat and unfold it.

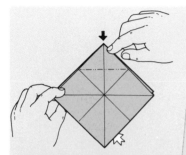

5 Here comes a sink. Unfold the preliminary fold, thereby flattening the top point.

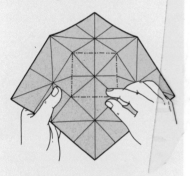

6 Crease the four sides of the inner square into mountain folds, so it looks like a table top. Push down on the middle of the square and at the same time . . .

7 push in the sides of the square, so they collapse towards the middle. Keep on pushing until the square fully collapses, thereby inverting the top point inside the top half of the preliminary fold.

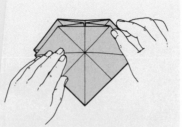

8 This is the completed sink. The quickest and easiest way to sink a point is to unfold the model completely, make the required mountain folds and then re-fold the model, thereby making the point disappear inside.

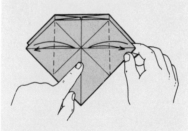

9 Valley fold the right- and left-hand side points into the middle. Press them flat and unfold them.

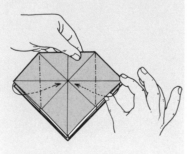

10 Inside reverse fold the side points along the fold-lines made in step 9.

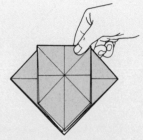

11 This should be the result.

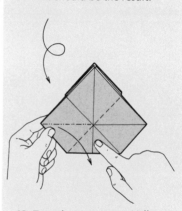

12 Turn the paper over. Valley fold the front flap of paper down on a line between the bottom left-hand corner and the middle of the 'upper' right-hand sloping edge, at the same time . . .

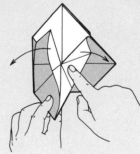

13 letting the inside layer rise up. Flatten the layer down and over to the left, at the same time flattening the front flap of paper down and over to the right.

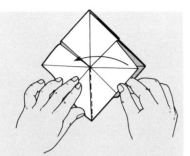

14 Valley fold the 'upper' right-hand side point over towards the left.

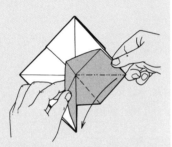

15 Valley fold the 'lower' right-hand side point down on a line between the bottom right-hand corner and the top of the sink, at the same time . . .

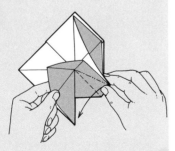

16 letting the inside layer rise up.

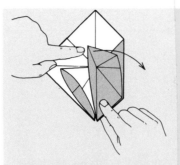

17 Flatten the layer down and . . .

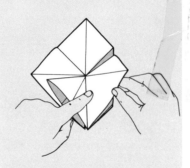

18 over to the right. Press the paper flat, making a triangular flap that points to the left.

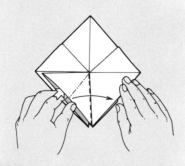

19 Open out the flap and squash it down neatly into a diamond.

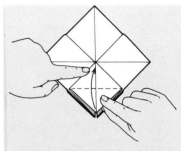

20 Valley fold the bottom point into the middle, thereby making a coloured triangle.

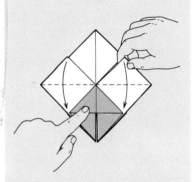

21 Valley fold the 'upper' right- and left-hand points down as shown.

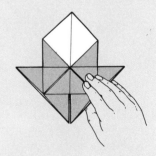

22 This should be the result.

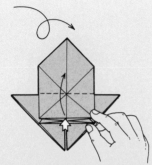

23 Turn the paper over. Valley fold the sink over, so it stands up into the air. Carefully open out . . .

24 the sink and . . .

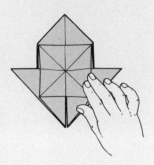

25 press it down neatly into a square.

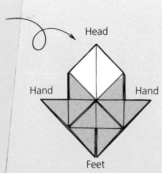

26 Turn the paper over. Here you can see which parts of the finished model the various points are going to be.

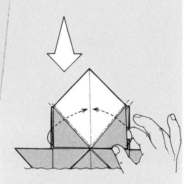

27 Inside reverse fold the two coloured triangles of the head section.

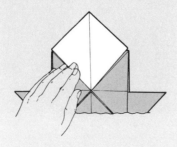

28 This should be the result.

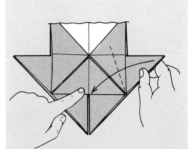

29 Starting in the middle of the right-hand sloping edge, valley fold the adjacent hand point over, so it lies along the coloured triangle's base.

30 Press the point only along this inside edge. Return it to its original position.

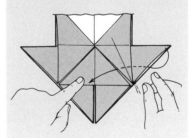

31 Inside reverse fold the point along the fold-lines made in step 30.

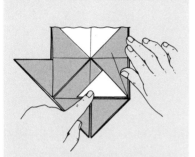

32 This should be the result. Press the paper flat.

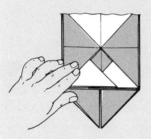

33 Repeat steps 29 to 32 with the left-hand sloping edge.

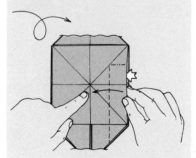

34 Turn the paper over. Valley fold the 'upper' right-hand side over to meet the middle fold-line, thereby making . . .

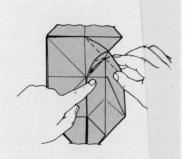

35 the sink's top right-hand corner rise up. Flatten the corner down and into the middle.

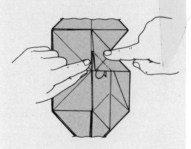

36 Mountain fold the corner in half.

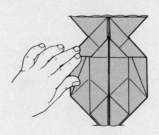

37 Repeat steps 34 to 36 with the left-hand side.

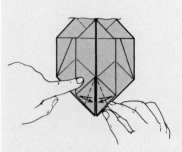

38 Starting in the middle of the feet section, valley fold the bottom points out as shown. Press them flat and unfold them.

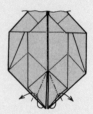

39 Inside reverse fold the points along the fold-lines made in step 38, to make . . .

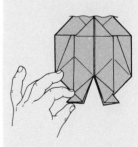

40 Father Christmas's feet.

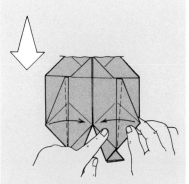

41 Valley fold the right- and left-hand flaps of paper over as shown.

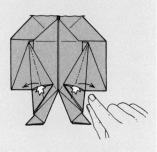

42 Open out the flaps and . . .

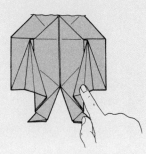

43 squash them down neatly. For a tidier look, tuck the squashed flaps underneath their adjacent layers of paper.

44 Turn the paper over. Open out the left-hand point, by valley folding its top layer of paper over as far as it will go.

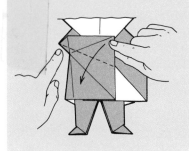

45 Valley fold the layer's top edge down as shown.

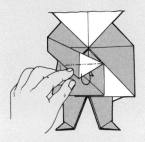

46 Mountain fold this point behind, thereby shaping the arm and sleeve.

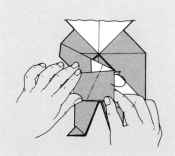

47 Mountain fold on a slant the top layer of paper, thereby shaping the hand.

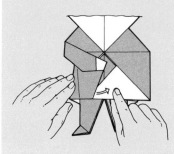

48 Release the right-hand point and open it out by valley folding its top layer of paper over as far as it will go. Now repeat steps 45 to 47.

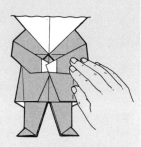

49 This should be the result.

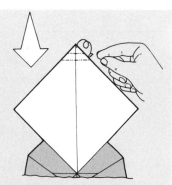

50 Mountain fold the head section's top point over and over a little.

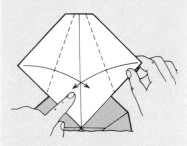

51 Valley fold the head section's upper sloping edges across, so they overlap a little.

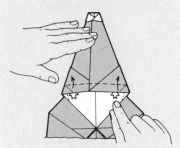

52 Valley fold the overlapping edges up as shown, at the same time forming a little squash fold on either side of the face.

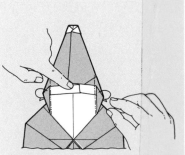

53 Mountain fold the squash folds, thereby shaping the face and hat.

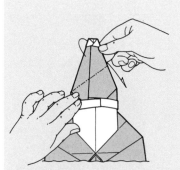

54 Mountain fold the top point outwards at an angle.

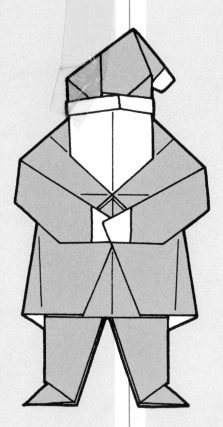

55 Here is the completed Father Christmas.

PANDA *(Steve Biddle)*

When two different pieces of origami are joined together, as with this delightful panda, the result is called compound origami. This technique is very useful for making animals, as you can fold the front half from one square and the rear half from another.

Use two squares of paper. For the panda's face the square should be three-quarters the size of the square used for the body. You will also need a tube of paper glue.

BODY

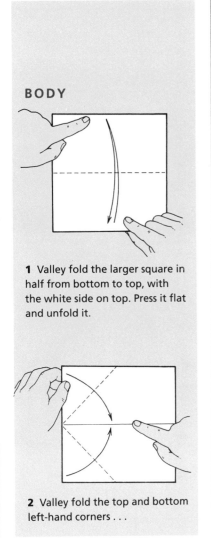

1 Valley fold the larger square in half from bottom to top, with the white side on top. Press it flat and unfold it.

2 Valley fold the top and bottom left-hand corners . . .

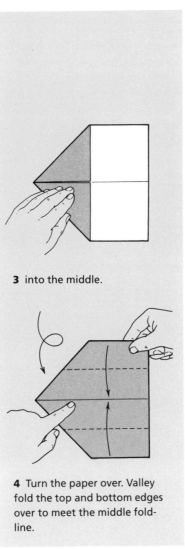

3 into the middle.

4 Turn the paper over. Valley fold the top and bottom edges over to meet the middle fold-line.

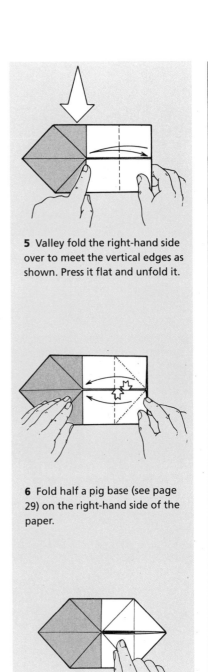

5 Valley fold the right-hand side over to meet the vertical edges as shown. Press it flat and unfold it.

6 Fold half a pig base (see page 29) on the right-hand side of the paper.

7 This should be the result.

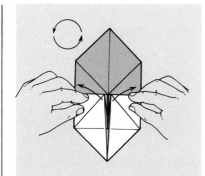

8 Turn the paper around. Pinch the two triangular points and pull them apart, until . . .

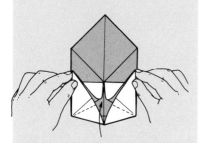

9 they are aligned with their adjacent sides, at the same time allowing the bottom point . . .

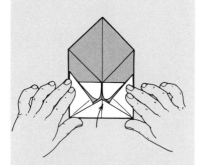

10 to rise up into a triangle. Press the paper down neatly.

11 Now prepare the triangle for a rabbit ear by valley folding its left-hand sloping edge down to meet the bottom edge. Press it flat and unfold it.

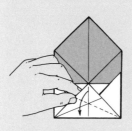

12 Repeat step 11 with the right-hand sloping edge, but do not unfold it.

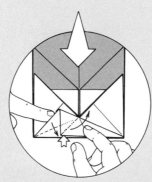

13 Pinch together the sloping edges along the fold-lines made in steps 11 and 12.

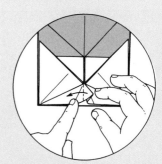

14 Valley fold the small triangular flap that appears over to one side, thereby . . .

15 completing the rabbit ear. This triangular flap is the panda's tail.

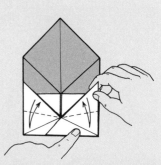

16 In preparation for an outside reverse fold, from the top of the tail, valley fold the triangular points down, so they meet their adjacent bottom corners. Press them flat and unfold them.

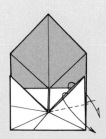

17 Outside reverse fold the right-hand triangular point. This is what you do. . . .

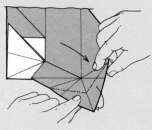

18 Partially open out the triangular point. Press down on the fold-lines made in step 16, to convert them into mountain folds.

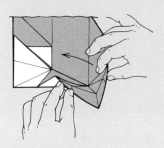

19 Bring the layers of the point back together, taking one to the front and one to the back, to . . .

20 complete the reverse fold. Valley fold it down as shown.

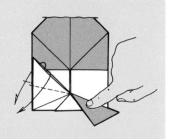

21 Repeat steps 17 to 20 with the left-hand triangular point.

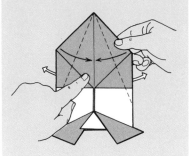

22 Valley fold the upper sloping edges over, so they lie along the vertical middle fold-line, at the same time . . .

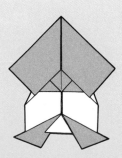

23 letting the corners flick up from underneath.

24 Turn the paper over. Valley fold the top point down on a line between the two side points. Press it flat and unfold it.

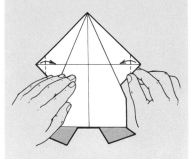

25 Valley fold a little of each side point inwards.

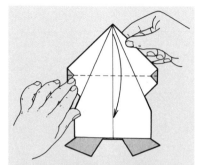

26 Valley fold the top point down and along the fold-line made in step 24.

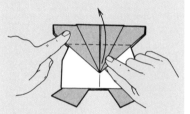

27 Valley fold the point up on a line between the two sloping edges as shown.

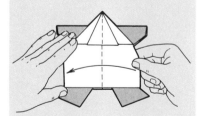

28 Valley fold the paper in half from right to left.

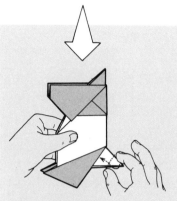

29 Blunt the tail's tip with an inside reverse fold.

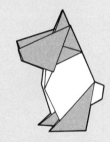

30 Here is the completed panda's body.

FACE

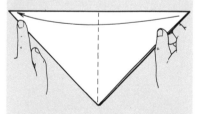

31 Begin with a diaper fold, coloured side up in step 1 (see page 50). Turn it around, so the tip is pointing towards you. Valley fold it in half from right to left, but do not press the paper completely flat.

32 Press down on the paper only a little, at this middle point. Unfold it.

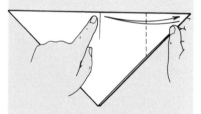

33 Valley fold the right-hand point over to meet the fold mark made in step 32. Again, do not press the paper flat, but only mark the quarter point. Return the point to its original position.

34 Finally, valley fold the right-hand point over to meet the fold mark made in step 33. Once again, do not press the paper flat, but only mark the eighth point. Return the point to its original position.

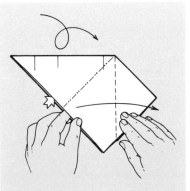

35 Valley fold the left-hand point over to meet the fold mark made in step 34. Press the paper flat.

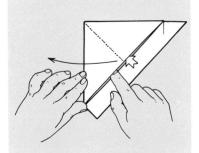

36 Open out the left-hand point and . . .

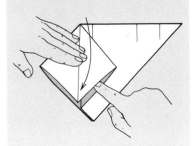

37 squash it down neatly into a diamond.

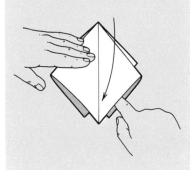

38 Turn the paper over. Repeat steps 36 . . .

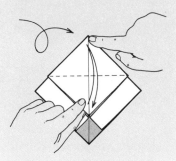

39 and 37, thereby making an off-centre preliminary fold.

40 Turn the paper over. Valley fold the front flap of paper in half from bottom to top. Press it only in the middle and unfold it.

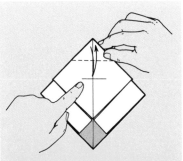

41 Valley fold the top point down to meet the fold-line made in step 40. Press it only in the middle and unfold it.

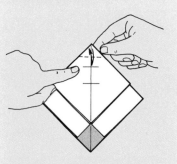

42 Valley fold the top point down to meet the fold mark made in step 41. Press it flat and unfold it.

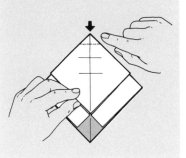

43 Sink the top point. This is what you do. . . .

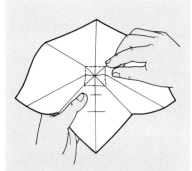

44 Unfold the paper, flattening the top. Crease the fold-lines made in step 42 into mountain folds.

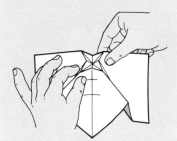

45 Push down on the middle of the square and at the same time push in the sides of the square, so they collapse towards the middle.

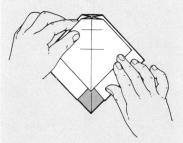

46 Keep on pushing until the square fully collapses, inverting the top point inside the off-centre preliminary fold.

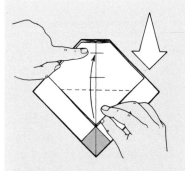

47 Valley fold the front flap of paper up to meet the fold mark made in step 41, thereby making a coloured triangle.

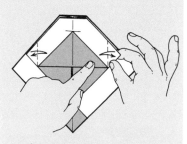

48 Valley fold the top right- and left-hand side points over to meet the edge of the triangle that is adjacent to them. Press them flat and unfold them.

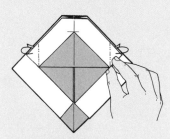

49 Mountain fold the side points behind and along the fold-lines made in step 48.

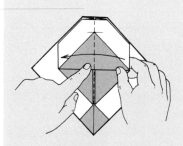

50 Valley fold the right-hand layer of paper to the left, as though turning the page of a book.

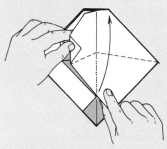

51 Valley fold the front flap of paper up as shown, so . . .

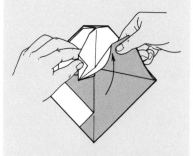

52 the bottom of its vertical fold-line meets the sink's top corner. At the same time, . . .

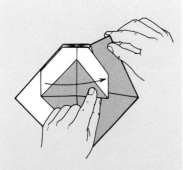

53 valley fold the right-hand layer of paper back to its original position. Valley fold the left-hand layer of paper to the right and repeat steps 51 to 53.

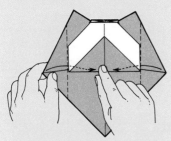

54 Valley fold the right- and left-hand side points over as shown, at the same time tucking them underneath the top layer of paper.

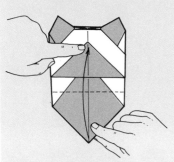

55 Valley fold the bottom point up to meet the fold mark made in step 41.

56 Valley fold a little of the top point's upper left-hand sloping edge down on a slant.

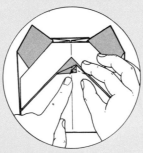

57 Repeat step 56 with the upper right-hand sloping edge, to make the panda's mouth.

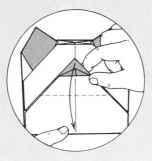

58 Treating them as if they were one, valley fold the mouth and the remaining top point down and along the fold-line made in step 40.

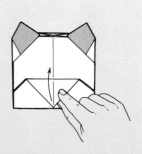

59 Return the top point to its original position.

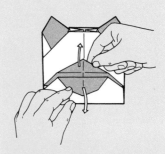

60 Gently pull the mouth and the top point apart.

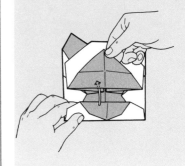

61 Tuck the mouth underneath the top point, locking the face section together.

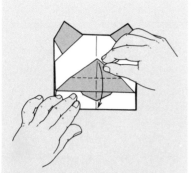

62 Valley fold the top point down and along the fold-line made in step 58.

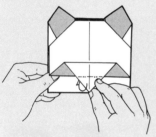

63 Mountain fold the point's tip up and inside the face section, to form the eyes.

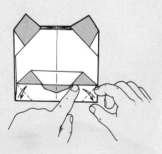

64 Valley fold the bottom corners over to meet the base of their adjacent eyes. Press them flat and unfold them.

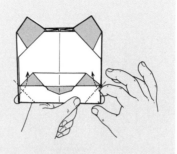

65 Inside reverse fold the bottom corners along the fold-lines made in step 64.

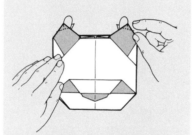

66 Shape the ears with mountain folds, to complete the face.

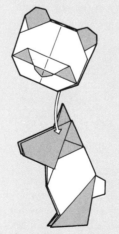

67 Glue the panda's face on to the body at an attractive angle.

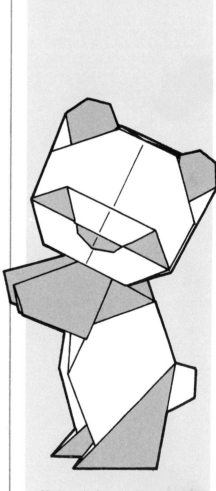

68 Here is the completed panda.

FLOWER (Traditional)

Many different flowers can be developed from the preliminary fold. If you repeated a similar kind of folding technique, such as a reverse fold, on each of its flaps, you could well be on the way to inventing your first origami flower.

Use a square of paper, coloured side up.

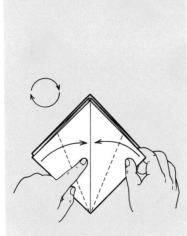

1 Begin with a preliminary fold (see page 124). Turn it around, so the open layers are pointing away from you. Valley fold the lower (folded) sloping edges over, so . . .

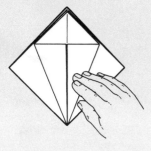

2 they lie along the middle fold-line.

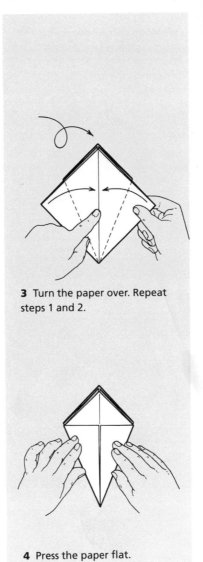

3 Turn the paper over. Repeat steps 1 and 2.

4 Press the paper flat.

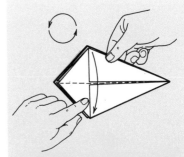

5 Turn the model around, so its open layers are pointing to the left. Valley fold it in half from top to bottom.

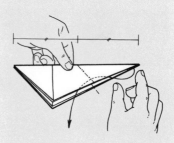

6 Inside reverse fold the right-hand point as far as shown, to make the stalk.

7 This shows step 6 taking place.

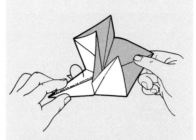

8 Turn the model around, so its open layers are pointing away from you. Pinch and . . .

9 peel back the top layer of paper as shown.

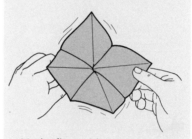

10 Mountain fold the stalk in half along its vertical length, thereby making . . .

11 the flower blossom outwards.

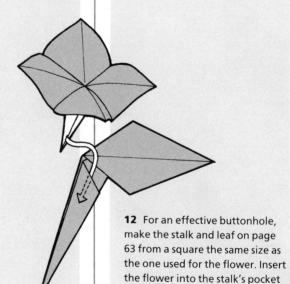

12 For an effective buttonhole, make the stalk and leaf on page 63 from a square the same size as the one used for the flower. Insert the flower into the stalk's pocket as shown.

BASKET *(Traditional)*

This model is very effective when made from a square of strong colourful paper, and is an ideal container for a special gift. The handle can be made shorter or longer.

Use two squares of paper, identical in size.

HANDLE

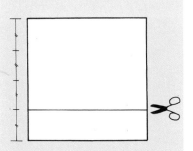

1 From one of the squares cut off a 4 x 1 strip as shown.

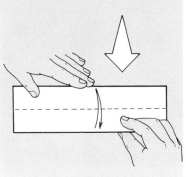

2 Place the strip sideways on, with the white side on top. Valley fold it in half from bottom to top. Press it flat and unfold it.

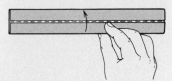

3 Valley fold the top and bottom edges over to meet the middle fold-line.

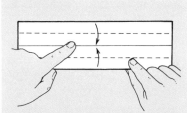

4 Valley fold the strip in half from bottom to top.

5 Here is the completed handle.

BASKET

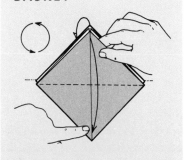

6 Begin with a preliminary fold (see page 124). Turn it around, so the open layers are pointing away from you. Valley fold the front flap of paper in half from top to bottom. Repeat behind.

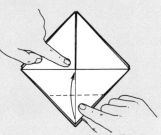

7 Valley fold the flap's tip into the middle, to make a traingle.

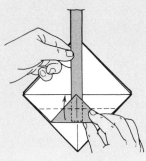

8 Insert one end of the handle underneath the triangle. Valley fold the triangle's bottom edge into the middle, thereby . . .

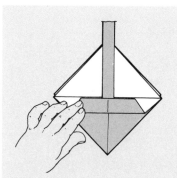

9 locking the handle in place.

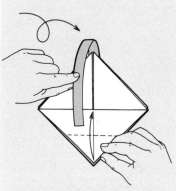

10 Turn the paper over. Bend the handle over the top. Repeat steps 7 to 9.

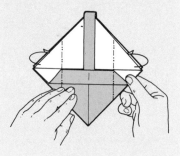

11 Mountain fold the right- and left-hand side points behind and into the middle.

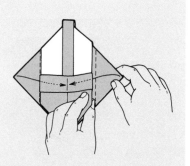

12 Repeat step 11, but valley fold instead.

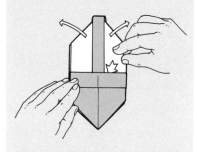

13 Pinch the side flaps and . . .

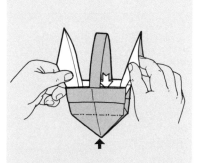

14 gently pull them apart, at the same time pushing down on the bottom point. The paper will open out into a basket.

15 Fold the side flaps into the basket. By pinching together the corners and sides of the basket, you can make it firm and strong.

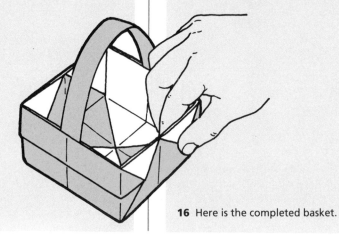

16 Here is the completed basket.

FROG BASE
(Traditional)

This is the second of the classic origami bases. If you look carefully at the crease pattern of an unfolded frog base, you can see that it is really just eight kite bases or a quadruple fish base. To make a frog base, use a square of paper, white side up, and follow the instructions overleaf.

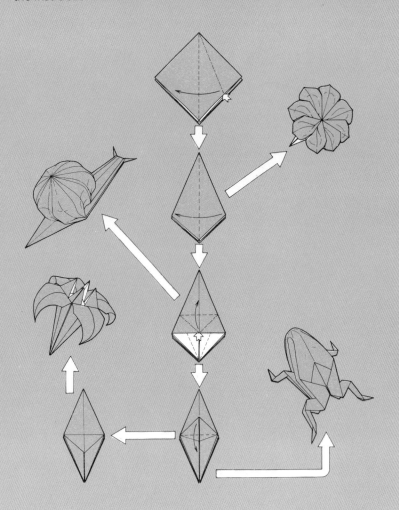

FROG BASE

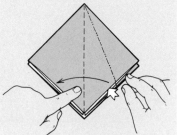

1 Begin with a preliminary fold (see page 124). Open out the right-hand flap of paper and . . .

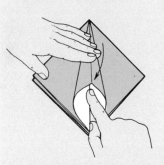

2 squash it down neatly into a diamond.

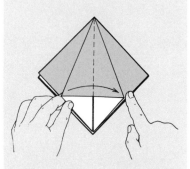

3 Valley fold the squashed flap in half from left to right.

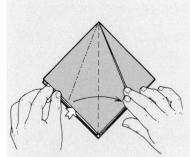

4 Repeat steps 1 and 2 with the left-hand flap of paper.

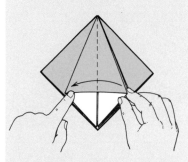

5 Valley fold the squashed flap in half from right to left.

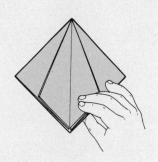

6 This should be the result.

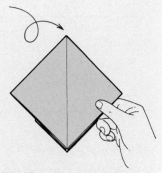

7 Turn the paper over. Repeat steps 1 to 5.

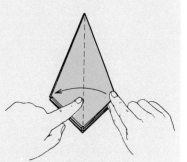

8 Valley fold the right-hand layer of paper over to the left. Repeat behind. You should now have four layers of paper on either side.

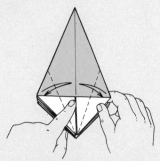

9 Valley fold the front flap's lower sloping edges over, so they lie along the middle fold-line. Press them flat and unfold them.

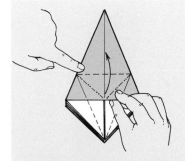

10 Pinch and lift up the flap's horizontal edge.

11 Continue to lift up the flap so its edges meet in the middle. Press the paper down neatly, making a small triangular flap.

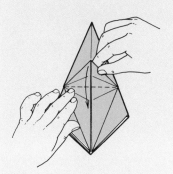

12 Valley fold the triangular flap down as far as it will go.

13 This should be the result. Repeat steps 9 to 12 with the remaining flaps.

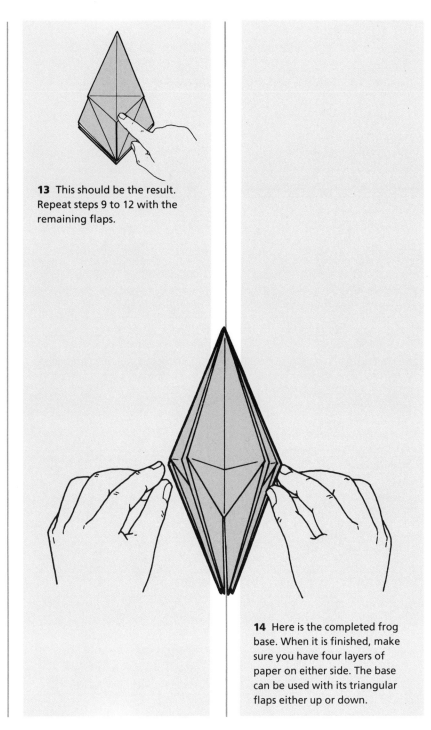

14 Here is the completed frog base. When it is finished, make sure you have four layers of paper on either side. The base can be used with its triangular flaps either up or down.

IRIS *(Traditional)*

By narrowing down the upper sloping edges of the frog base we are able to create the narrow leaves of the iris. Some paperfolders call this model the lily, and thus the frog base becomes the lily base.

Use a square of paper, white side up.

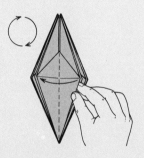

1 Begin with a frog base (see page 146). Turn it around, so the small triangular flaps are pointing away from you. Valley fold the right-hand layer of paper over to the left, as if turning the page of a book. Repeat behind.

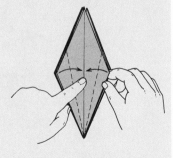

2 Valley fold the front flap's lower sloping edges over, so they lie along the middle fold-line.

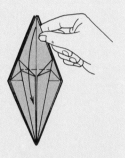

3 Valley fold the top point down as far as it will go.

4 This should be the result. Repeat steps 1 to 3 with the remaining flaps.

5 Lift the side flaps up slightly.

6 Repeat step 5 with the top and bottom flaps, so the paper becomes three-dimensional.

7 Curve the flaps by rolling each one around your finger. This completes the iris.

FROG *(Traditional)*

This is the model that gave its name to the frog base. The frog is a very good lesson in the technique of inside reverse folding. Use a square of paper (preferably green in colour), white side up.

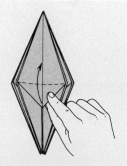

1 Begin with a frog base (see page 146). Valley fold the small triangle up as far as it will go.

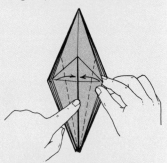

2 Valley fold the front flap's lower sloping edges over so they lie along the vertical middle line.

3 This should be the result. Repeat steps 1 and 2 with the remaining flaps.

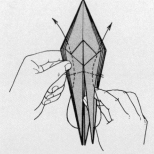

4 Inside reverse fold the front two bottom points up as far as they will go.

5 Inside reverse fold the remaining bottom points out to either side.

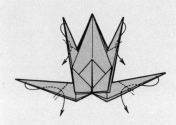

6 Now inside reverse fold each of the four points, to make the frog's legs.

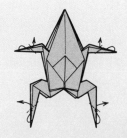

7 Finally, inside reverse fold each of the points again, to make the feet.

8 Hold the paper very loosely and blow gently into the small hole you will find at the bottom, to make the paper inflate.

9 Turn the model over, completing the frog. If you place the frog on a flat surface and run a finger firmly down his back, he will jump about.

CARNATION
(Mitsunobu Sonobe)

The tricky part of this model comes towards the end when it is opened out and the petals are being shaped.

Use a square of paper, coloured side up.

CARNATION

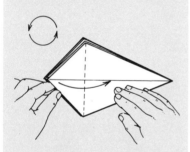

1 Begin with a completed step 7 of the frog base (see page 146). Turn it around so the open layers are pointing to the left. Valley fold the left-hand flap of paper over towards the right on a line between the top and bottom points.

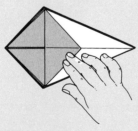

2 This should be the result. Repeat with the remaining flaps.

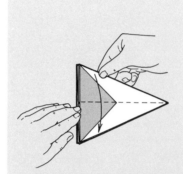

3 Valley fold the paper in half from top to bottom.

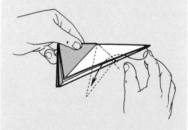

4 Inside reverse fold the right-hand point into the position shown by the dotted lines.

5 Turn the carnation around and open it out by pinching and . . .

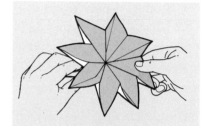

6 peeling back the top layer of paper, to reveal the petals.

7 Turn the carnation upside down. Hold a petal between your thumb and forefinger. Push into the petal's back and make a slight indentation, at the same time opening it out. Repeat with the remaining petals, at the same time trying to wedge them tightly together.

8 Turn the paper over. This completes the carnation.

SNAIL *(Traditional)*

For some strange reason, this very lifelike model is relatively unknown here in the West. The snail is a very good lesson in the technique of opening out a folded point.

Use a square of paper, white side up.

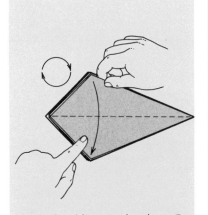

1 Begin with a completed step 7 of the frog base (see page 146). Turn it around so the open layers are pointing to the left. Valley fold the front flap of paper in half from top to bottom, thereby revealing the 'underneath' squash fold.

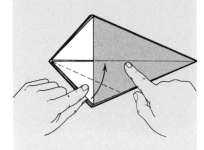

2 Valley fold the lower left-hand sloping edge over, so it lies along the middle fold-line.

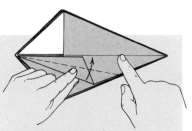

3 Once again, valley fold the lower left-hand sloping edge over, so it lies along the middle fold-line.

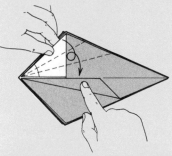

4 Valley fold the upper left-hand sloping edge over twice on its way to lie along the middle fold-line.

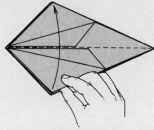

5 Valley fold the folded layer and the next flap of paper in half from bottom to top, revealing the 'underneath' squash fold.

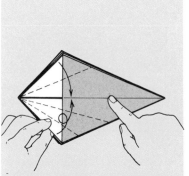

6 Be careful here! Repeat step 2 with the upper left-hand sloping edge and repeat step 4 with the lower left-hand sloping edge.

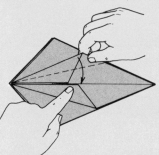

7 Repeat step 3 with the upper left-hand sloping edge.

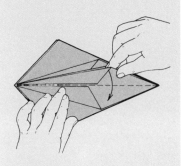

8 Valley fold the folded layer in half from top to bottom.

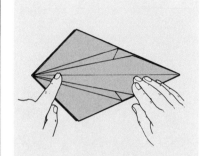

9 This should be the result.

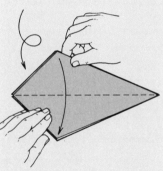

10 Turn the paper over. Valley fold the front flap of paper in half from top to bottom, revealing the 'underneath' squash fold.

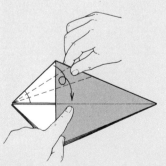

11 Repeat step 4.

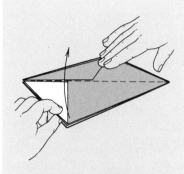

12 Valley fold the front flap of paper and the adjacent one in half from bottom to top.

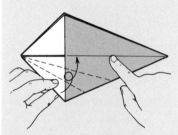

13 Repeat step 4 with the lower left-hand sloping edge.

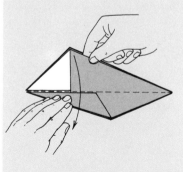

14 Valley fold the front flap of paper in half from top to bottom.

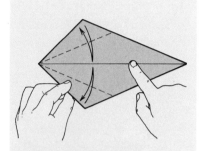

15 Valley fold the upper and lower left-hand sloping edges over, so they lie along the middle fold-line. Press them flat and unfold them, thereby preparing the paper for a petal fold.

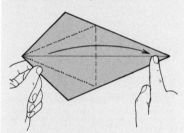

16 Pinch and lift up the left-hand point's tip.

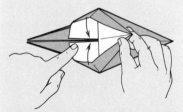

17 Continue to lift up the point so its edges meet in the middle. Press the paper flat and to the right, thereby making it diamond-shaped and completing the petal fold.

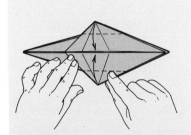

18 Valley fold the top and bottom points into the middle.

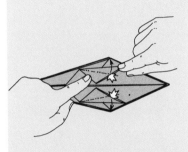

19 Open out and squash the points down neatly, so . . .

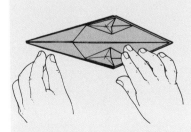

20 they become aligned with the left-hand sloping edges as shown.

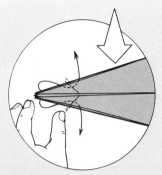

21 Inside reverse fold the top and bottom left-hand points out to either side, to make the snail's antennae.

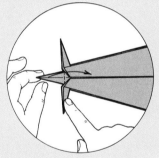

22 Valley fold the remaining left-hand point over on a line between the two antennae.

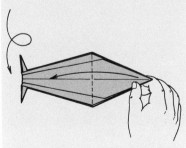

23 Turn the paper over. Lift the multi-layered right-hand point up into the air on a line between the top and bottom points.

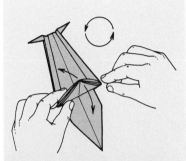

24 Turn the snail around so its tail is pointing towards you. Begin to inflate the upright point by pulling gently on its edges.

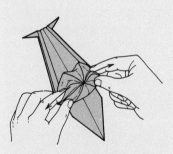

25 Continue the inflation of the point, to make the snail's shell.

26 Here is the completed snail.

BIRD BASE
(Traditional)

This is the last of the classic origami bases, and is thought by many paperfolders to be the keystone to origami. If you look carefully at the crease pattern of an unfolded bird base, you can see that it is really just a quadruple kite base. This shows that the relationship between the classic bases (fish, frog and bird) is one of folding edges to diagonal fold-lines and making narrow points stem from the corners of a square. Knowing this, you can use these points to make ears, legs, petals, wings and so on. When making your own models, study the number of points that the various bases have to offer and their positions within a particular base, then pick the base which has the number you feel is suitable for your creation.

To make a bird base, use a square of paper, white side up, and

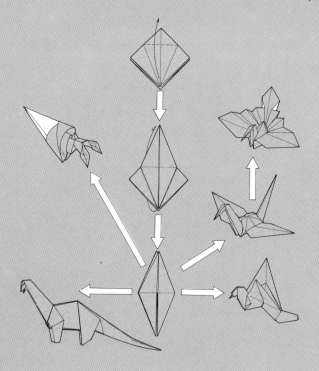

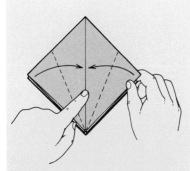

1 Begin with a preliminary fold (see page 124). Valley fold the lower (open) sloping edges over, so they lie along the middle fold-line.

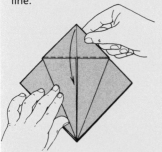

2 The paper should now look like an ice cream cone, with a triangle of ice cream at the top and the cone below. Valley fold the 'ice cream' down and over the cone.

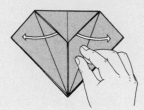

3 Unfold the edges from underneath the 'ice cream', as if opening the doors of a cupboard. Now make a petal fold. This is what you do. . . .

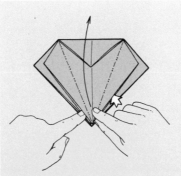

4 Pinch and lift up the front flap of paper.

5 Continue to lift up the flap, so . . .

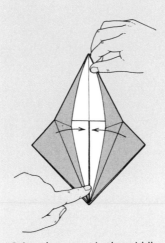

6 its edges meet in the middle.

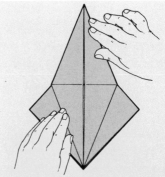

7 Press the paper flat, thereby making it diamond-shaped. This completes the petal fold.

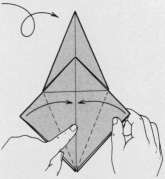

8 Turn the paper over. Valley fold the lower (open) sloping edges over, so they lie along the middle fold-line. Repeat steps 2 to 7, thereby completing . . .

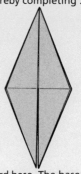

9 the bird base. The base comes in two forms, either as here, or with its top flaps valley folded down in front and behind.

CRANE *(Traditional)*

Among Japanese paperfolders the bird base is known as the crane base. That is because this model is well known throughout Japan. Use a square of paper, white side up.

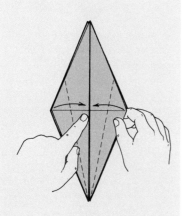

1 Begin with a bird base (see page 155). Valley fold the lower sloping edges over, so . . .

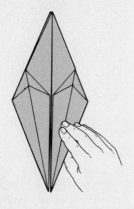

2 they lie along the vertical middle line.

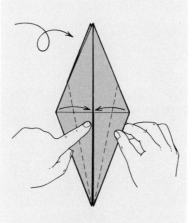

3 Turn the paper over. Repeat steps 1 and 2.

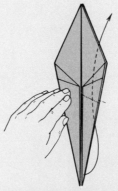

4 Make the crane's head and tail by inside reverse folding the bottom points. This is what you do. . . .

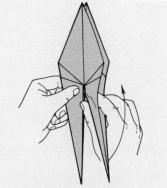

5 Pinch a bottom point and . . .

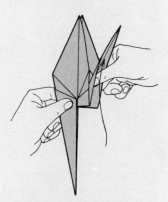

6 pull it up inside the model.

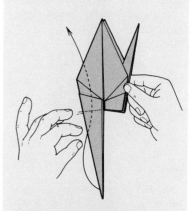

7 Press the point flat into this position. Repeat steps 5 to 7 with the remaining bottom point.

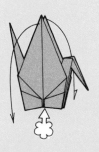

8 Inside reverse fold the tip of one of the top points, to make the crane's head and beak.

9 Pick up the crane and inflate it by blowing gently into the small hole that you will find at the bottom, at the same time pulling the wings apart and flattening out the middle point a little.

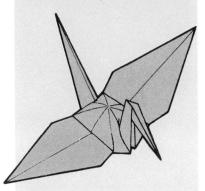

10 Here is the completed crane.

FLAPPING BIRD *(Traditional)*

Who the creator of this magical piece of origami is remains a mystery. We have added a few cosmetic folds here and there to make the bird look more realistic.

Use a square of paper, white side up.

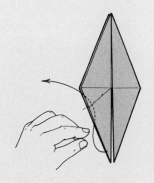

1 Begin with a bird base (see page 155). Inside reverse fold the bottom left-hand point into the position shown in step 2, to make the bird's tail.

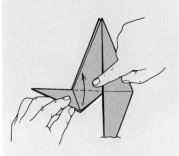

2 Open out the tail.

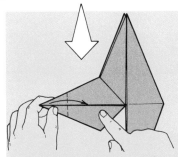

3 Blunt the tip of the tail with a valley fold.

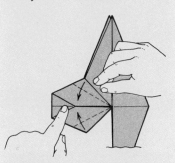

4 Valley fold the top and bottom points over as shown, to shape the base of the tail.

5 Valley fold the tail in half from top to bottom.

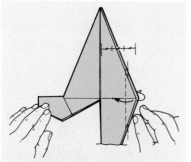

6 Valley fold the right-hand side point over as shown. Repeat behind.

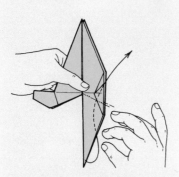

7 Inside reverse fold the remaining bottom point into the position shown in step 8.

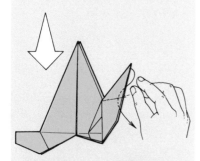

8 Inside reverse fold the point's tip, thereby making the bird's head.

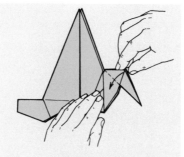

9 Open out the head.

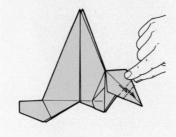

10 Step fold the head as shown to make the beak.

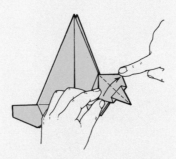

11 Valley fold the head in half from bottom to top.

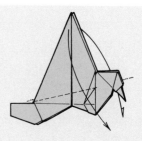

12 Softly valley fold the front wing down and towards the head. Repeat behind.

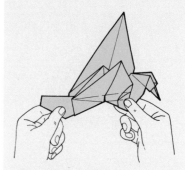

13 Here is the completed flapping bird.

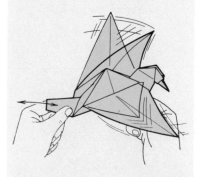

14 Hold the bird's chest, pull the tail and the wings will flap!

KOTOBUKIZURU
(Congratulations Crane)
(Traditional)

Very often it is possible to discover a new and better way of folding a particular model. When we first folded the kotobukizuru there was a very nasty 'turn inside out' move when making its tail, but following the first few steps you can see how we have tried to make this much easier. As a rule, it is better to choose a simple way of illustrating or teaching a particular folding technique than a more complex one, thereby giving the folder the opportunity to make a model successfully rather than give up in frustration.

Use a square of paper, white side up.

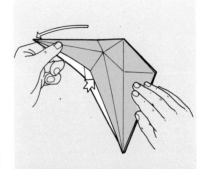

5 opening out its inner layers of paper. Press the paper down neatly . . .

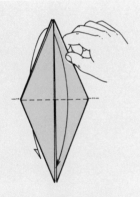

1 Begin with a bird base (see page 155). Valley fold the top flaps down in front and behind.

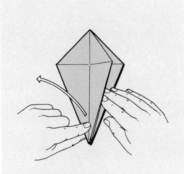

3 With one hand, lift up the front flap and with the other hold down firmly the bottom right-hand layers of paper.

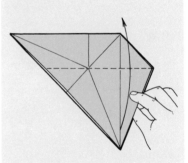

6 into this position. Valley fold the front flap of paper up on a line between the right-hand side point and where the fold-lines intersect on the left.

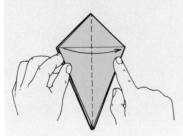

2 Valley fold the left-hand layer of paper over to the right, as if turning the page of a book.

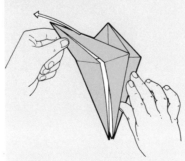

4 Pull the front flap to the left, thereby . . .

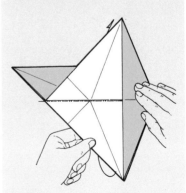

7 Repeat step 6 behind.

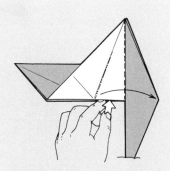

8 Open out the left-hand layer of paper from the bottom, thereby puffing . . .

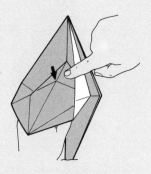

9 outwards its upper sloping edges. From the top flatten the inside ridge of the paper down neatly, at the same time . . .

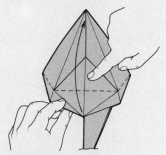

10 valley folding the bottom point up to meet the top points. Press the paper flat.

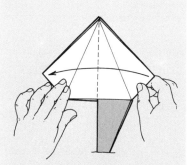

11 Valley fold the top right-hand layer of paper over to the left.

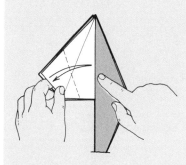

12 Valley fold the top left-hand layer of paper over to meet the middle fold-line. Press it flat and unfold it.

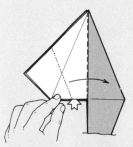

13 Open out the top left-hand layer from the bottom, thereby puffing . . .

14 outwards its upper sloping edges. From the top, flatten the 'inside' ridge of paper. Finally press the paper down neatly.

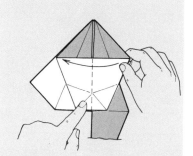

15 Valley fold the top right-hand layer of paper over towards the left.

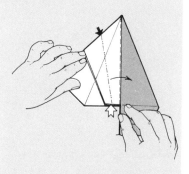

16 Repeat steps 12 to 14.

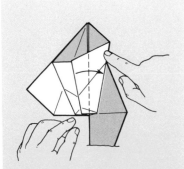

17 Valley fold the top left-hand layer of paper over to the right.

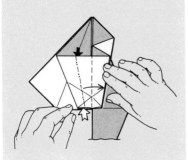

18 Repeat steps 12 to 14 with the top left-hand layer of paper.

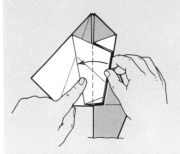

19 Valley fold all the flattened right-hand layers of paper over towards the left.

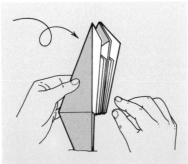

20 Turn the paper over. Repeat steps 12 to 19 with the top right-hand layer of paper.

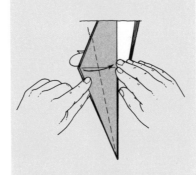

21 Narrow down the bottom point with a valley fold. Repeat behind.

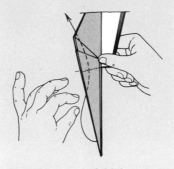

22 Inside reverse fold the bottom point into the position shown in step 23.

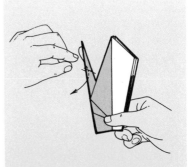

23 Inside reverse fold the point's tip, to make the crane's head and beak.

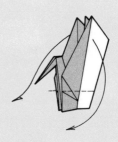

24 Fan out the wings.

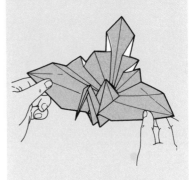

25 Here is the completed kotobukizuru. In Japan this model is folded when congratulations are given, such as at New Year or at a wedding.

HERMIT CRAB (*Shozo Ishida*)

One is not restricted to folding models from one particular base, as it is sometimes possible to combine the bases. This model is made from a combination of the bird and frog bases.

Use a square of paper, white side up.

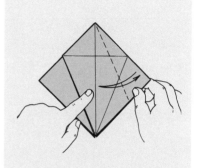

5 Valley fold the upper right-hand sloping edge over, so it lies along the middle fold-line. Press it flat and unfold it.

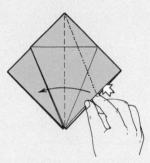

6 Open out the right-hand flap of paper and squash it down neatly into a diamond.

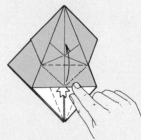

7 Pinch and lift up the squashed flap's horizontal edge. Continue to lift up the flap, so its edges meet in the middle. Press the paper down neatly, thereby making a small triangular flap.

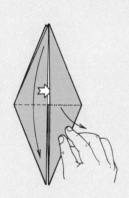

1 Begin with a bird base (see page 155). Unfold the right-hand layer of the front flap, at the same time . . .

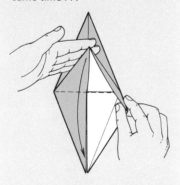

2 valley folding the flap's tip down . . .

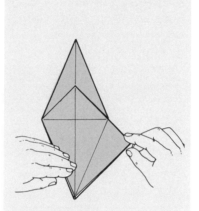

3 to meet the bottom points.

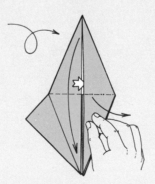

4 Turn the paper over. Repeat steps 1 to 3.

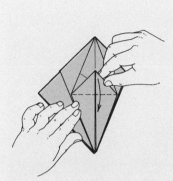

8 Valley fold the triangular flap down as far as it will go.

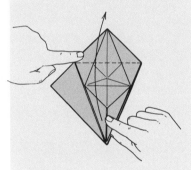

9 Valley fold the bottom points up on a line between the two side points.

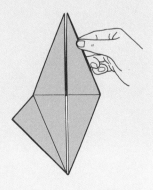

10 This should be the result.

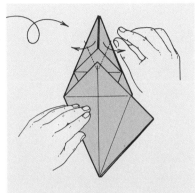

11 Turn the paper over. Valley fold the two top points out to either side as shown, thereby making the crab's front pincers.

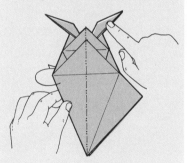

12 Mountain fold the paper in half from left to right.

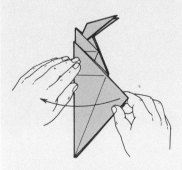

13 Valley fold the right-hand layer of paper over to the left.

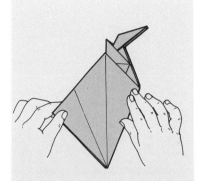

14 This should be the result.

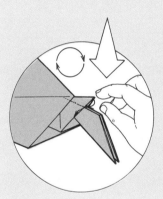

15 Turn the paper around. Inside reverse fold the small right-hand point into the position shown in step 16.

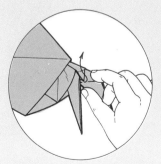

16 Now reverse fold the point back out, so it protrudes above the pincers.

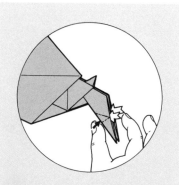

17 Open out and indent the pincers slightly, so . . .

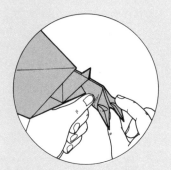

18 they become three-dimensional.

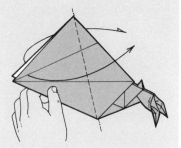

19 Valley fold the left-hand layer of paper over to the right on a line between the top and bottom points. Repeat behind.

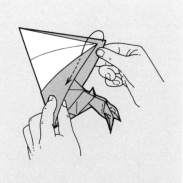

20 Tuck one top layer of paper deep inside the other, so making a cone.

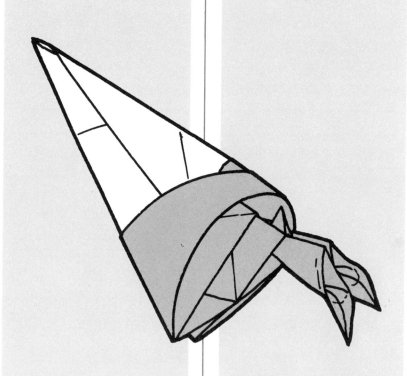

21 Here is the completed hermit crab.

APATOSAURUS
(Seiji Nishikawa)

As we have already said, many paperfolders like to fold a single theme, and this folder is no exception. He has combined his love of origami with a knowledge of dinosaurs to produce a collection of prehistoric animals. Here is one of them.

Use a square of paper, white side up.

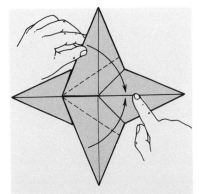

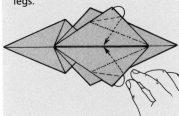

5 Valley fold the top and bottom flaps over and towards the right, so they lie along the horizontal middle line. These are the front legs.

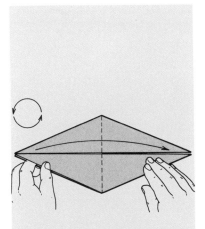

1 Begin with a bird base (see page 155). Turn it around so the flaps point to the left. Valley fold the front flap in half from left to right.

2 Turn the paper over. Valley fold the bottom point over and towards the left, so it lies along the horizontal middle line and at the same time . . .

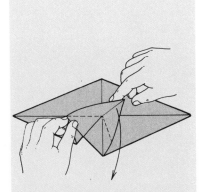

3 makes the adjacent right-hand point rise up. Press the upright point down neatly.

4 Repeat steps 2 and 3 with the top point.

6 Working from their tips, narrow down the front legs by mountain folding the paper along the existing fold-lines as shown. The valley fold-line is made when the paper has been flattened down into position.

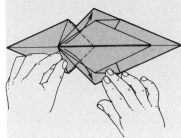

7 Valley fold the left-hand flaps of paper out as far as they will go, thereby making the back legs.

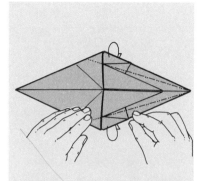

8 Mountain fold the upper and lower sloping edges of the right-hand flap on a line between its tip and the base of each front leg.

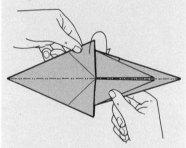

9 Mountain fold the paper in half from top to bottom.

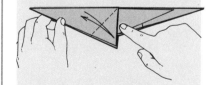

10 Valley fold the left-hand half of the top edge down, so it lies along the front edge of the back leg. Press it flat and unfold it.

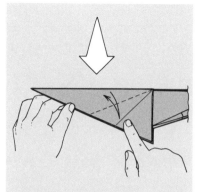

11 Valley fold the left-hand half of the top edge down, so it lies along the fold-line made in step 10. Press it flat and unfold it.

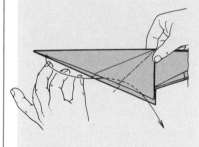

12 Along the fold-lines made in step 10, inside reverse fold the left-hand half of the top edge into the model.

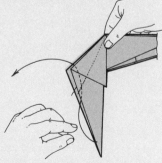

13 Along the fold-lines made in step 11. reverse fold the left-hand half of the top edge back out.

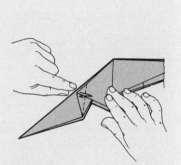

14 Valley fold the triangular area behind the back leg in half. Press it flat and unfold it.

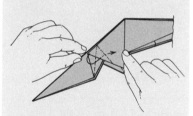

15 Repeat step 14, but this time push the triangular area inwards as shown by the mountain fold-line, to . . .

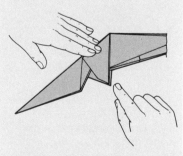

16 shape the back leg. Repeat steps 14 to 16 behind.

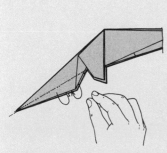

17 Narrow down the left-hand point with a mountain fold. Repeat behind, thereby making the tail.

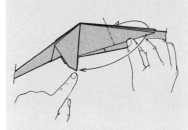

18 Valley fold the front leg over to meet the tip of the back leg. Repeat behind.

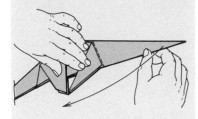

19 Start to shape the neck by valley folding the right-hand point down, so it lies on top of the front leg.

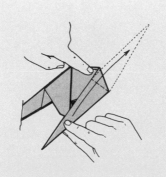

20 Valley fold the point into the position shown by the dotted lines.

21 Unfold the last two folds.

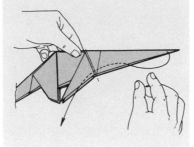

22 Inside reverse fold the right-hand point along the fold-lines made in step 19.

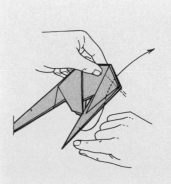

23 Reverse fold the point back out . . .

24 along the fold-lines made in step 20.

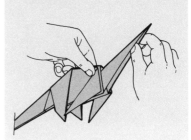

25 This should be the result.

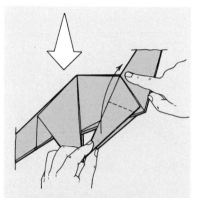

26 Valley fold the front leg up and towards the neck.

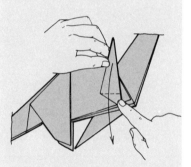

27 Valley fold the front leg down as shown. Unfold the last two folds.

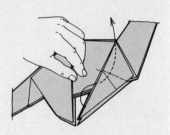

28 Inside reverse fold the front leg along the fold-lines made in step 26.

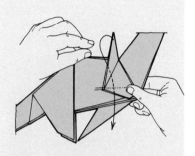

29 Reverse fold the leg back down along the fold-lines made in step 27.

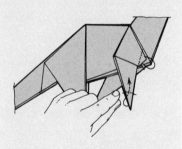

30 Blunt the tip of the leg with an inside reverse fold. Shape the thigh with a mountain fold.

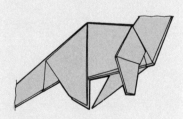

31 This should be the result. Repeat steps 26 to 30 behind.

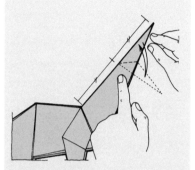

32 Valley fold the neck's top point down as far as shown. Press it flat and unfold it.

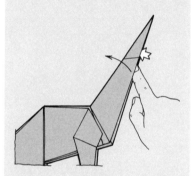

33 Open out the neck.

34 Working on the inside of the neck, valley fold the tip down to meet the bottom of the V-shaped fold-lines.

35 Valley fold the tip up to meet the top edge, thereby making a small pleat in the paper.

36 Valley fold the neck in half from side to side.

37 Inside reverse fold the neck along the fold-lines made in step 32, thereby making the head.

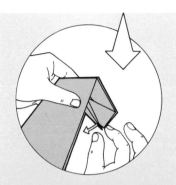

38 Pull the tip down slightly, to suggest the lower jaw.

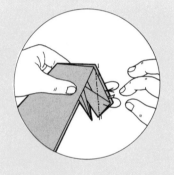

39 Shape the head with a mountain fold. Repeat behind.

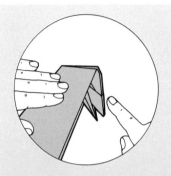

40 This should be the result.

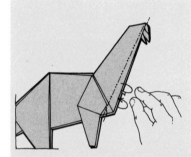

41 Shape the neck with a mountain fold. Repeat behind.

42 Indent the tail slightly, to complete the apatosaurus.

RECTANGULAR AND MODULAR ORIGAMI

Origami models are not just folded from squares; they can be made from any other regular (or irregular) shape. Some paperfolders even use a circle! For example, John Cunliffe, a well known British origami artist, specializes in folding wallets, envelopes and a whole range of other useful items from rectangular paper.

Modular origami consists of folding simple non-representational shapes or units and fitting them together to build more complex constructions. The units can be glued or held together by interlocking them: present-day paperfolders prefer the latter method. In Japan this style of paperfolding is known as 'unit origami'.

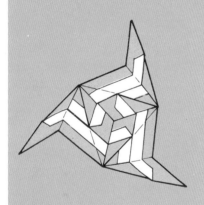

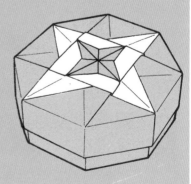

WALLET *(John Cunliffe)*

You will find this model ideal for carrying pens, pencils and business cards.

Use a rectangle of paper, about A3 in size, white side up.

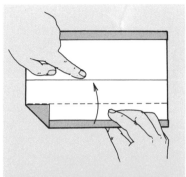

5 Once again, valley fold the bottom edge up to meet the middle fold-line.

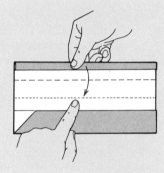

6 Valley fold the top edge down and towards the middle fold-line.

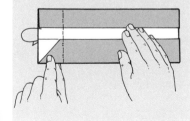

7 Mountain fold the left-hand side as shown.

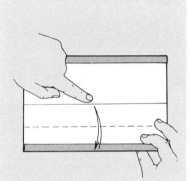

3 Valley fold the bottom edge up to meet the middle fold-line. Press it flat and unfold it.

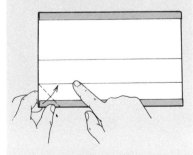

4 Valley fold the bottom left-hand corner over to meet the adjacent fold-line.

1 Place the rectangle sideways on. Valley fold a little of the top and bottom edges over.

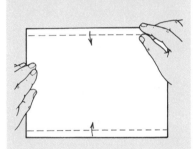

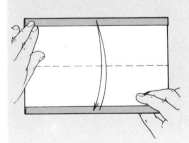

2 Valley fold the paper in half from bottom to top. Press it flat and unfold it.

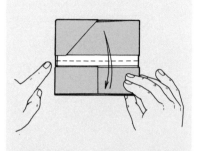

8 Turn the paper over. Valley fold the paper in half from side to side. Press it flat and unfold it.

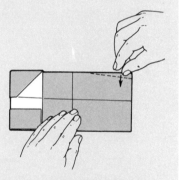

9 Valley fold a little of the top right-hand corner down on a slant.

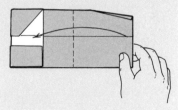

10 Valley fold the paper in half from right to left, at the same time . . .

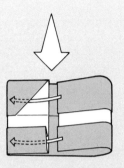

11 inserting the right-hand side deep into the left-hand layers of paper.

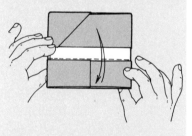

12 Valley fold the bottom rectangle of paper up. Press it flat and unfold it.

13 Depending upon how thick you wish your finished wallet to be, valley fold the top edge down. (The thicker the fold, the smaller the spine.) Press it flat and unfold it.

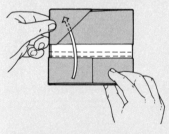

14 Using the fold-lines made in steps 12 and 13, shape the wallet's spine and insert the bottom left-hand corner underneath the opposite sloping edge as shown.

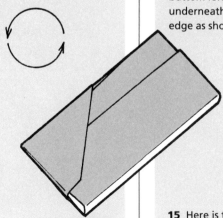

15 Here is the completed wallet.

BASIC UNIT *(Steve Biddle)*

The following two models are all folded from this basic unit. Once the unit has been mastered it is a very easy item to use as a construction piece when making solid geometrical shapes.

Use a square of paper, white side up.

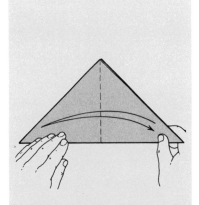

1 Begin with a diaper fold (see page 50). Valley fold it in half from side to side. Press it flat, then unfold the paper completely.

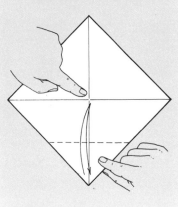

2 Valley fold the bottom corner into the middle. Press it flat and unfold it.

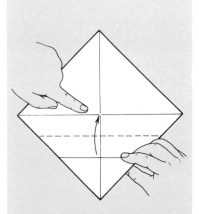

3 Valley fold the bottom corner up, so the fold-line made in step 2 lies along the horizontal fold-line and makes a coloured triangle.

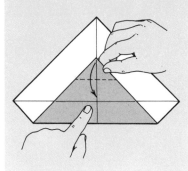

4 Valley fold the triangle's top point to meet the intersection of the fold-lines as shown.

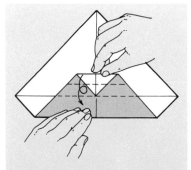

5 Valley fold the newly-made edge over and over as shown.

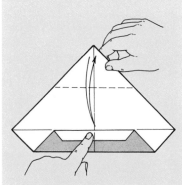

6 Valley fold the top corner down to meet the horizontal fold-line. Press it flat, then unfold it.

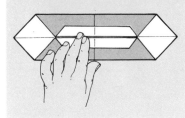

7 Repeat steps 3 to 5 with the top corner.

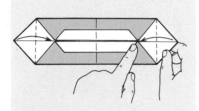

8 Valley fold the right- and left-hand corners in as shown, so the paper looks like a rectangle.

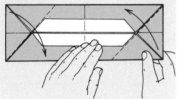

9 Valley fold the right-hand side up, so it lies along the top edge, and valley fold the left-hand side down, so it lies along the bottom edge.

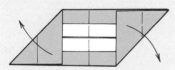

10 Press the sides flat and unfold them.

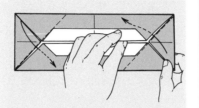

11 Repeat step 9, but tuck the right-hand side underneath the top layer of paper, and the left-hand side underneath the bottom layer.

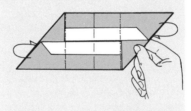

12 Mountain fold the top and bottom triangular points along their vertical edge.

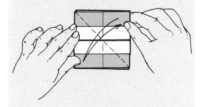

13 Valley fold in half from top right to bottom left. Press the paper flat and then let it open out a little.

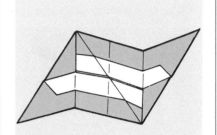

14 Here is the completed basic unit.

MULTI-UNIT SPHERES
(Traditional)

For a creative challenge, try folding the 12-piece multi-unit sphere out of three colours of paper and the larger sphere out of five colours, then constructing them so that no two adjacent 'pyramids' are of the same colour.

Use 12 squares of paper, identical in size, white side up.

5 Insert the fifth unit in place, thereby making another pyramid.

TWELVE-PIECE MULTI-UNIT SPHERE

1 Begin by folding each square into a basic unit (see page 173). Insert one unit inside another as shown.

2 Insert another unit in place, thereby making . . .

3 a pyramid. The pyramid is the keystone both to this sphere and the 30-piece one.

4 Insert the fourth unit in place.

6 Insert the sixth and seventh units in place, thereby making two more pyramids. By now you have constructed half the sphere.

7 Insert the remaining units in place by rotating the sphere as you do so. The result should be . . .

8 a further four pyramids. Make sure that all the units are tightly fitted together.

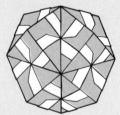

9 Here is the completed 12-piece multi-unit sphere.

It is even possible to build up a much larger sphere using 30 squares of paper.

10 Begin with a completed step 5. Make three more pyramids (step 3) and . . .

11 insert them all together, so they form a circle. Carry on inserting units around this circle and forming them into pyramids, so . . .

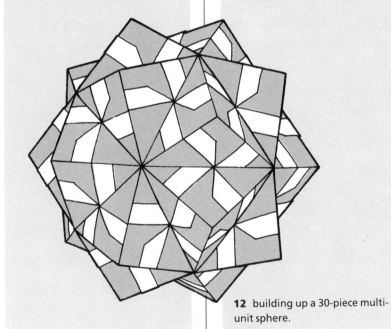

12 building up a 30-piece multi-unit sphere.

OCTAGONAL BOX *(Tomoko Fuse)*

This paperfolder specializes in making unit boxes, and her creations come in all shapes and sizes. Folding the various units is very simple, and joining them together just requires a little patience. For a creative challenge, try folding the units in a variety of colours and joining the parts together in a different way than the one illustrated here. You will be amazed at how many patterns can be produced.

Use eight squares of paper, identical in size, white side up.

LID

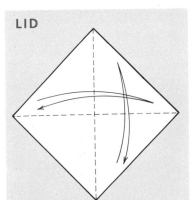

1 Turn one square around to look like a diamond. Valley fold and open up the opposite corners together in turn to mark the diagonal fold-lines.

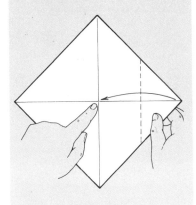

2 Valley fold the right-hand corner into the middle.

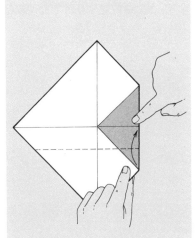

3 Valley fold the bottom right-hand side point up, so . . .

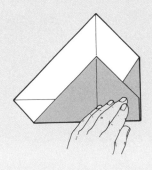

4 it meets the middle of the right-hand side.

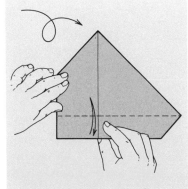

5 Turn the paper over. Valley fold the bottom edge up and along the existing horizontal fold-line. Press it flat and unfold it.

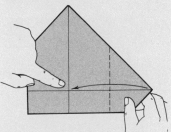

6 Valley fold the right-hand corner over to where the fold-lines intersect.

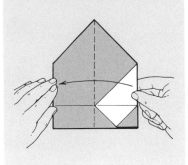

7 Valley fold the paper in half from right to left.

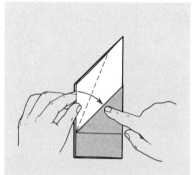

8 Valley fold the top left-hand layer of paper down . . .

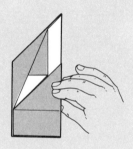

9 to lie along the sloping edge as shown.

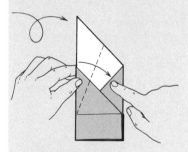

10 Turn the paper over. From the left-hand end of the horizontal fold-line, valley fold the left-hand edge down to lie along the right-hand sloping edge as shown.

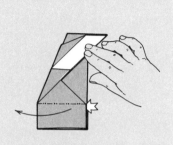

11 Open out the paper by taking the top right-hand layer across to the left, so the model becomes three-dimensional.

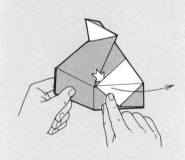

12 Pull the inner flap of paper across . . .

13 to the right.

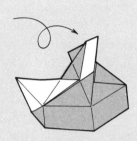

14 Turn the model over. This completes one unit of the lid. Now make three more such units.

JOINING THE UNITS TOGETHER

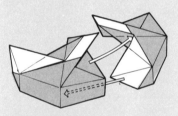

15 Insert the white flap of one unit deep into the side pocket of another.

16 Lock both units together by tucking the point of the top unit underneath the point of the bottom unit.

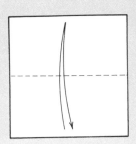

17 Repeat steps 15 and 16 with the remaining units.

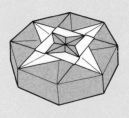

18 Here is the completed lid.

BASE

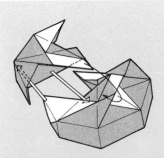

19 Valley fold a square in half from bottom to top. Press it flat and unfold it.

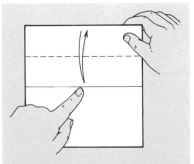

20 Valley fold the top edge down to meet the middle fold-line. Press it flat and unfold it.

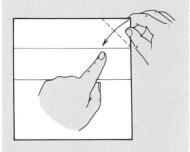

21 Valley fold the top right-hand corner over to meet the adjacent fold-line.

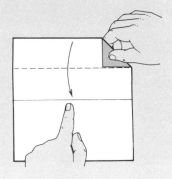

22 Once again, valley fold the top edge down to meet the middle fold-line.

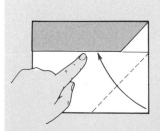

23 Valley fold the bottom right-hand corner up to meet the horizontal fold-line as shown.

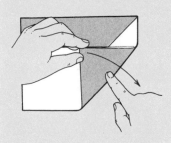

24 Press the corner flat and unfold it.

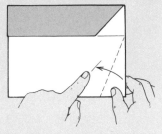

25 From the right-hand end of the horizontal fold-line, valley fold the bottom right-hand corner over to meet the adjacent fold-line, thereby making a triangle.

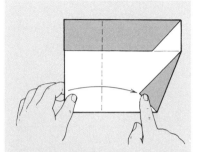

26 Valley fold the left-hand side over to meet the tip of the newly made triangle.

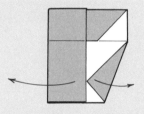

27 Press the paper flat and unfold steps 25 and 26.

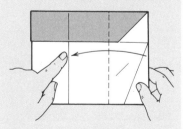

28 Valley fold the right-hand side over to meet the fold-line made in step 26.

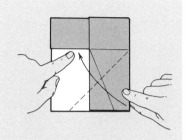

29 Repeat step 23.

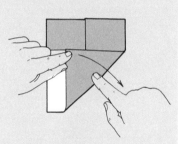

30 Repeat step 24.

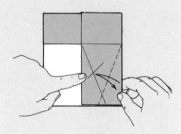

31 From the right-hand end of the horizontal fold-line, valley fold the bottom right-hand corner over to meet the fold-line made in steps 29 and 30. Press it flat and unfold it.

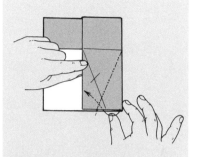

32 Inside reverse fold the lower right-hand corner along the fold-lines made in step 31.

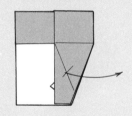

33 Unfold the right-hand layer of paper.

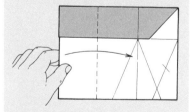

34 Refold the left-hand side of the paper along the fold-line made in step 26.

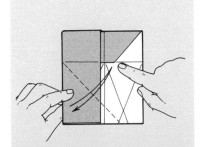

35 Repeat steps 23 and 24 with the bottom left-hand corner.

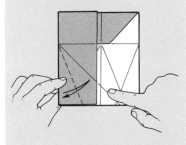

36 From the left-hand end of the horizontal fold-line, valley fold the bottom left-hand corner over to meet the fold-line made in step 35. Press it flat, then unfold it .

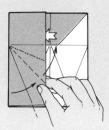

37 Step fold the top left-hand layer of paper by placing the valley fold made in step 35 . . .

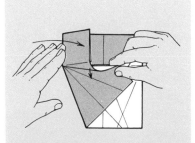

38 along the horizontal fold-line as shown. Press the paper flat.

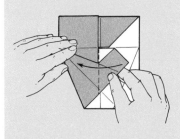

39 Valley fold the right-hand half of the step fold over to the left.

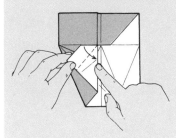

40 Valley fold the top layer of the step fold down, so its top edge lies along the adjacent vertical edge and makes a small flap as shown.

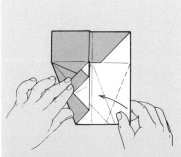

41 Refold step 25.

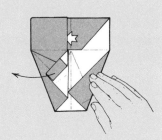

42 Open out the paper by folding the top left-hand layer across to the left, so the model becomes three-dimensional.

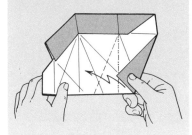

43 Step fold the right-hand section of paper along the existing fold-lines as shown, to . . .

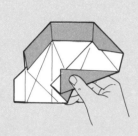

44 complete one unit of the base. Now make three more such units.

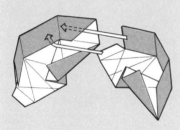

JOINING THE UNITS TOGETHER

45 Insert one unit deep into the side pocket of another and tuck its flap (see step 40) between the pocket's front and back layers.

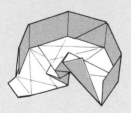

46 This should be the result.

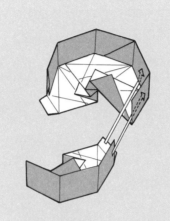

47 Repeat step 45 with the remaining units.

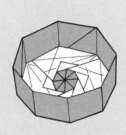

48 Here is the completed base.

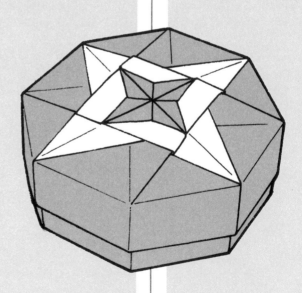

49 Slide the lid over the base, completing the octagonal box.

SENBAZURU AND CRAB (*Traditional*)

The folding method for the following kirikomi models was originally published in a Japanese book called *Senbazuru Orikata* (*How to Fold a Thousand Cranes*) in 1797. The author, Gido Rokoan (1759-1831), was the head priest at a temple called Choenji in Kuwana City, near Nagoya. His philosophy behind the title of Senbazuru was that if one crane represents a thousand years of happiness, then a hundred cranes would equal one hundred thousand years of happiness and so a thousand cranes would mean one million years of happiness. Sadly, only five original copies of Gido Rokoan's book still exist.

The kirikomi technique involves slits being made in a piece of paper to produce a number of mutually connected squares. These squares are then folded into cranes. According to the way the paper is cut, you can arrange the cranes into a chain, linked together beak to beak, or wing tip to wing tip, and so on: the list is endless. Some present-day paperfolders have used the Senbazuru technique to combine other models. For example, Toshie Takahama, a well-known Japanese origami artist, has created an origami lei. As a creative challenge, see which models in this book would be ideal for the Senbazuru approach.

The crab, on the other hand, is based upon one that appears in a collection of 50 small volumes of Japanese memoranda called 'Kan-no-mado' (Japanese for 'window of the coldest season' or 'mid-winter window'). The Kan-no-mado was copied in manuscript by Kazuyuki Adachi from a work by Gido Rokoan (and perhaps other sources) and was compiled in 1845. The single volume on origami contains 49 examples of ceremonial and play origami, all of them illustrated with brush drawings. This one volume is regarded as a classic on origami.

IMOSEYAMA
(Sisters)
(Traditional)

In all the following models, the corner of the square that contains an 'O' means that when a crane is folded, this corner should become the head and beak. In the advance Senbazuru models it may help to mark these corners in pencil before any cutting and folding takes place.

Use a rectangle of paper, 2 x 1 in proportion, white side up.

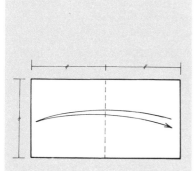

1 Place the rectangle sideways on. Valley fold it in half from side to side. Press it flat and unfold it.

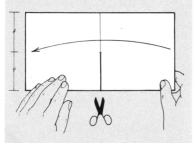

2 Cut along the middle fold-line as far as shown. Valley fold the paper in half from right to left.

3 Valley fold the paper in half from top left to bottom right, thereby making a diaper fold.

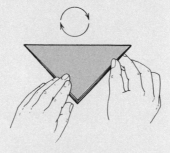

4 Turn the diaper fold around so it points towards you. Treating the double layers as if they were one, fold them into a bird base (see page 155).

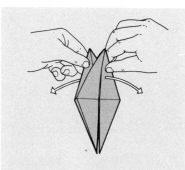

5 Gently tease the bird base apart and unfold the paper . . .

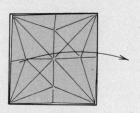

6 back to the original rectangle.

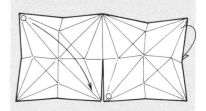

7 Following the existing fold-lines . . .

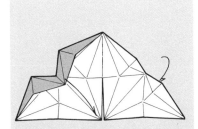

8 carefully form the paper . . .

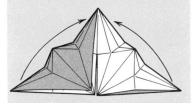

9 into two bird bases, one of which . . .

10 is coloured and the other white.

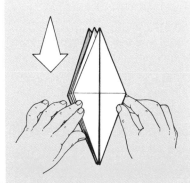

11 The bases should be joined together at one of their upper flaps. Fold them into cranes (see page 156).

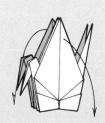

12 Being careful not to tear the paper, gently open out the cranes.

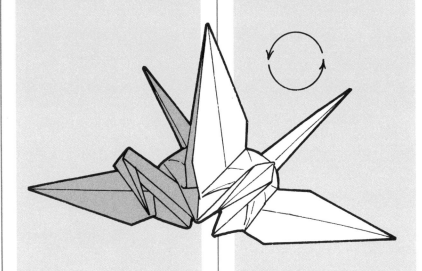

13 Here is the completed Imoseyama.

INAZUMA *(Lighting) (Traditional)*

Use a rectangle of paper, 3 x 1 in proportion, white side up. Divide the paper into three squares. Cut as shown, being careful not to go through the top and bottom edges. Then fold each of the squares into a crane. The result will be three cranes joined together by wing to tail and head to wing.

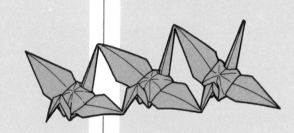

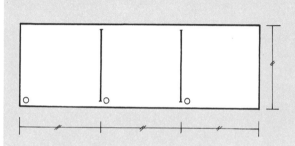

MEGUMI *(Blessing)* *(Megumi Biddle)*

Use a square of paper, white side up. Divide the sides into quarters. Cut as shown, to make one large square and twelve smaller ones. Fold the larger square first and then the smaller ones into cranes. The result will be a circle of small cranes, with a larger crane suspended across the middle.

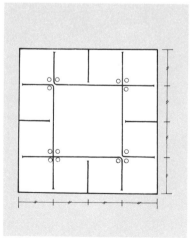

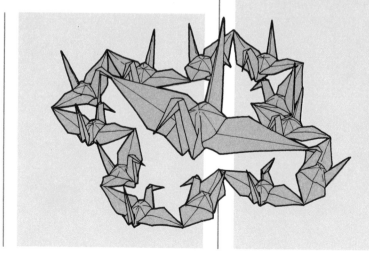

CRAB
(Traditional)

Even though this model may appear daunting at first it is actually very easy to fold. Remember, as with any model, to fold neatly and look very carefully at each illustration to see what you should do.

Use a large square of thin, but strong paper, coloured side up.

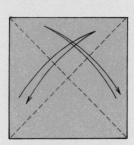

1 Valley fold the opposite corners together in turn to mark the diagonal fold-lines, then open up again.

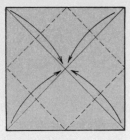

2 Fold a blintz base (see page 95).

3 This should be the result.

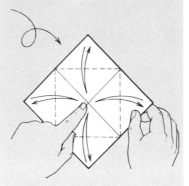

4 Turn the paper over. Blintz once again. Press it flat and unfold it.

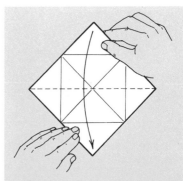

5 Valley fold the paper in half from top to bottom, thereby making a triangle, the tip of which points towards you.

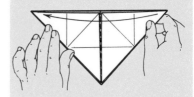

6 Valley fold the triangle in half from right to left.

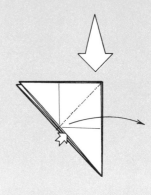

7 Lift the top half up along the middle fold-line. Open out the paper . . .

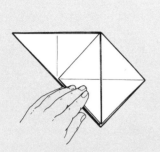

8 and squash it down neatly into a diamond.

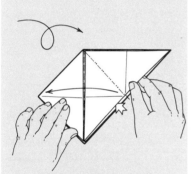

9 Turn the paper over. Repeat steps 7 and 8, thereby making . . .

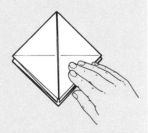

10 a blintzed preliminary fold. Unfold the paper completely.

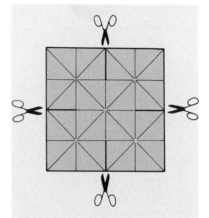

11 From the middle of each edge cut towards the middle of the paper as far as shown.

12 Carefully reform the blintzed preliminary fold.

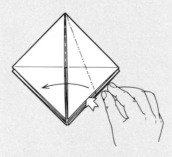

13 Open out the right-hand flap of paper and . . .

14 squash it down neatly into a diamond.

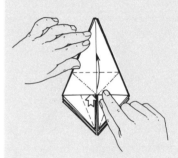

15 Petal fold the front flap (see steps 9 to 11 of the frog base on pages 145-147).

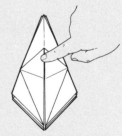

16 Repeat steps 13 to 15 with the remaining three flaps, thereby making a blintzed frog base.

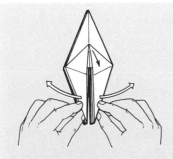

17 Slightly unfold the blintzed frog base.

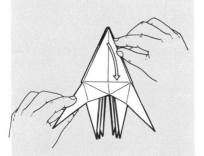

18 Gently release the top layer of paper and . . .

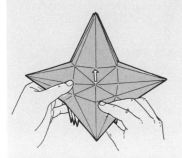

19 bring it down towards you, but do not press the paper flat.

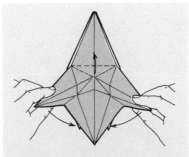

20 Following the existing fold-lines, flatten down . . .

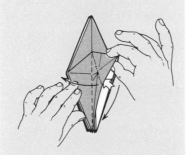

21 and squash the shaded flap.

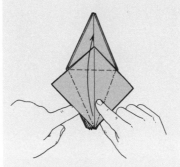

22 Petal fold the front flap (see steps 4 to 7 of the bird base on page 155).

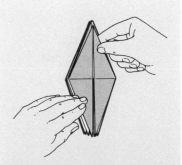

23 This should be the result. Repeat steps 17 to 22 with the remaining three layers of paper, thereby making . . .

24 a quadruple bird base. You can also fold this base without having to make the cuts shown in step 11. When you have finished, make sure there are eight layers of paper on either side.

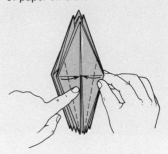

25 Be careful here! Valley fold the front flap's lower sloping edges over, so . . .

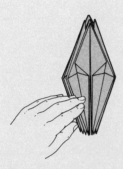

26 they lie along the vertical middle line. Repeat steps 25 and 26 behind and on the sides.

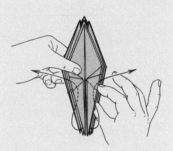

27 Inside reverse fold the eight bottom points out to either side.

28 Again reverse fold the eight points, to make the crab's legs.

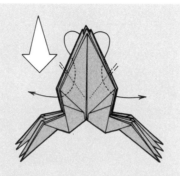

29 Inside reverse fold the two inner points out to either side.

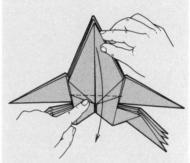

30 Valley fold the front flap down as far as it will go, thereby revealing the multi-layered middle point.

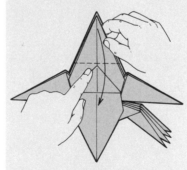

31 Valley fold the multi-layered point down on a horizontal line that runs adjacent to the tip of the visible triangle.

32 Valley fold the point up to lie along the horizontal edge, so it points towards the right. Press it flat and unfold it.

33 Valley fold the point up to lie along the horizontal edge, so it points towards the left. Press it flat and unfold it.

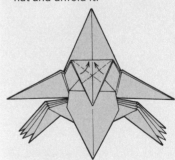

34 Pinch together the two sides of the point along the fold-lines made in steps 32 and 33, thereby making a rabbit ear that points to the left.

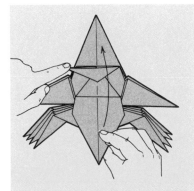

35 Valley fold the lower flap of paper up as far as it will go and . . .

36 repeat steps 31 to 34 with it, but make the rabbit ear in step 34 point to the right. These rabbit-eared flaps are the crab's eyes. Valley fold the remaining flap of paper down and . . .

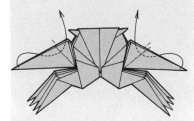

37 tuck it underneath the front legs. Inside reverse fold the two side points as shown.

38 Outside reverse fold the two side points, to make the crab's claws.

39 Outside reverse fold the legs.

40 Open out the claws and eyes, so they become slightly three-dimensional.

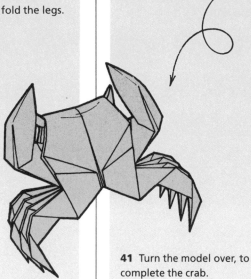

41 Turn the model over, to complete the crab.

INDEX